BORN
many
TIMES

Also by George McMullen

BORN
many
TIMES

George McMullen

HAMPTON ROADS
PUBLISHING COMPANY, INC.

for the evolving human spirit

Cover design by Marjoram Productions
Cover art by John Edens
Illustrations by Abraham Truss

For information write:

Hampton Roads Publishing Company, Inc.
134 Burgess Lane
Charlottesville, VA 22902

Or call: 804-296-2772
FAX: 804-296-5096

e-mail: hrpc@hrpub.com
Web site: http://www.hrpub.com

If you are unable to order this book from your local
bookseller, you may order directly from the publisher.
Quantity discounts for organizations are available.
Call 1-800-766-8009, toll-free.

Library of Congress Catalog Card Number: 99-71622

ISBN 1-57174-131-3

10 9 8 7 6 5 4 3 2 1

Printed on acid-free recycled paper in the United States

THIS BOOK IS DEDICATED TO

My wife Charlotte

and my children Elizabeth, Dennis, and Cindy,

where all my love exists.

ACKNOWLEDGMENTS

I want to thank Ann Emerson, who has given so much of her time and editorial experience to all of my books so far. She has been a close friend of my family, as was her husband, Norman.

I cannot forget my good friend Abraham Truss, who has drawn the sketches that have appeared in my books. He is a man with many talents and has proven to be a good friend. It was he and my wife Charlotte who decided that I should write this book. So you can blame them.

Thanks also to these people who have supported me and given so freely their friendship and advice: Raymond Worring, Whitney Hibbard, Jim Robbins, Patrick Marsolek, Stephen Schwartz, Marshal Payne, and Britt and Lee Elders.

CONTENTS

FOREWORD

There is a place where time makes no sense, where distance and space have no bearing to what we accept, and where things are known that defy what civilization has learned about how things are known. This place is the mind of the psychic. Without personally experiencing or thoroughly researching psychic phenomena, there is no way of justifying belief in psychic phenomena since it belies what we have learned, especially that which we've been taught from ninth grade science class up through any bachelor of science degree.

For more than a century scientists have used controlled laboratory methods to investigate "abnormal" experiences and energy effects. These have been labeled clairvoyance, telepathy, precognition and psychokinesis, and millions of test incidents have been dutifully recorded. But how are psychic events properly replicated in the laboratory? The police can't find a body. A psychic is engaged and takes them right to it, with no previous knowledge of the case or the region. How is a laboratory procedure devised to duplicate the find? It has been so difficult that orthodox scientists find it hard to give credibility to the psychic phenomena since the tools that they use in their work cannot suit those used for the paranormal.

But there is hope now with the development of what are called meta-analytic techniques and concepts whereby a quantitative assessment can be made of cumulative evidence. Scientific work now shows empirical proof: psychic phenomena exist.

Science has no explanation for why these phenomena exist, nor do the psychics, but that is not to say that the majority of mainstream scientists accept or deny their existence; they just cannot identify with them and don't know what to make of them, and make an unconscious decision to let them go by. They simply don't pay them any attention. Such was certainly the case for this writer.

All these experiments, however, would have been unnecessary if they had known George McMullen. You wouldn't need a laboratory to ascertain psychic phenomena—just talk with George for awhile. His most notorious accomplishments were reported by the paranormal investigator Stephen Schwartz in his book, *The Secret Vaults of Time*.

Schwartz recounts years of work by the eminent Canadian archaeologist, Dr. J. Norman Emerson, who took George to a number of sites to find or learn of things unknown to archaeology. As archaeologists are famous for doing, Emerson recorded everything meticulously. Bottom line: Emerson computed George's accuracy at 80 percent! Even an accuracy rating of eight percent should have raised the fever of every archaeologist in the world.

It was during these site visits that George encountered what he called spirit guides: Red Snake, Running Bear, Two Faces, and now this one, Born Many Times. The spirits talk with George, who merely relates what they say to us. Hard to believe? Well, yes. But then knowing George, I can imagine no other way by which he could have known so many ways of these Native Americans from centuries ago. The reader ought to keep this in mind while reading *Born Many Times*.

Marshall Payne
Tampa, Florida

Marshall Payne is an engineer, a graduate of
Massachusetts Institute of Technology

INTRODUCTION

Professor J. Norman Emerson, one of the revered "fathers of Canadian archaeology," senior archaeologist and professor of anthropology at the University of Toronto, founding vice-president and former president of the Canadian Archaeological Association, addressed his colleagues at the annual convention of the Canadian Archaeological Association at the Simon Fraser University in British Columbia as follows:

> It is my conviction that I have received knowledge about archaeological artifacts and archaeological sites from a psychic informant who related this information to me without any evidence of the conscious use of reasoning. . . . By means of the intuitive and parapsychological, a whole new vista of man and his past stands ready to be grasped.

A year later, at the insistence of Margaret Mead, the American Anthropological Association sponsored, for the first time, a symposium on parapsychology and anthropology. At the symposium Professor Emerson argued for bringing "the parapsychology and anthropology together into a meaningful study of human prehistory," which, he believed, "will lead to a richer, and hopefully a more accurate understanding of human prehistory."

It is to this end that George McMullen, Professor Emerson's psychic informant, has written a series of books published by Hampton Roads that culminated in this current volume. It is George's purpose to help fulfill Professor Emerson's wish for "a richer, and hopefully a more accurate understanding of human prehistory." What better way, George believes, than to have eyewitness accounts from someone who was there. Such a witness is Born Many Times, a spirit entity who claims, as his name suggests, to have lived many lifetimes, some of which he tells us about through the person of George McMullen.

My twenty years' association with George began while doing research for my book, "Psychic Criminology", and culminated in a comprehensive case study of him as part of my doctoral work in psychology under Stanley Krippner, Ph.D. During this association I have been consistently impressed not only with George's psychic abilities, but with his honesty, integrity, and sincerity. George is definitely not your stereotypical psychic; in fact, he actually intensely dislikes being referred to as one.

It has taken a great deal of courage for George to "go public," for which he has suffered much criticism and has not been given the credit he is due.

Those of us who cannot see the world as he does, however, are much enriched by his second sight and his willingness to boldly share what has been disclosed to him. For those not fortunate enough to actually spend time with George in the field observing him do psychic or intuitive archaeology as I have (which often is an astounding experience), *Born Many Times* (and George's other books) is the next best thing.

Whitney S. Hibbard
author, with Raymond W. Worring,
Psychic Criminology and Forensic Hypnosis

BORN *many* TIMES

THE SHAMAN

1. THE SHAMAN

Passages related by the author are denoted in italic typeface. Born Many Times' and Grey Fox's words appear in roman.

It was dark in the lodge. Smoke hung in the air from the fire which burned in the pit in the center of the room. The men sat in a circle around the fire pit. The shaman had been summoned by the chief and his council to discuss a problem that had arisen the previous day, and they awaited his coming.

The shaman arrived and took his place beside the chief and listened as the problem was discussed. A group of white settlers had moved into a nearby valley that was considered to be a sacred place by the tribal members. Young warriors from the tribe were at this time meeting at a secret place to make plans to attack the white settlers.

The chief explained that this was being done without the permission of the council or himself. They knew that to attack these people would make them very angry and would cause the tribe to suffer in the future. They knew the white people had many soldiers and guns.

The chief asked those assembled if they had any solution to the problem. No one appeared to know what to do because they knew the young warriors would not listen to any of them.

The shaman said he would speak with the warriors and see if somehow he could cool them down and reason with them. This pleased those present. They knew no one had the respect of the young people as much as he had. They asked if it was possible that he could find the secret place where they were gathering. The shaman answered that he would have no trouble finding them. He knew where they had gathered. No one questioned this because they realized the shaman always knew where people were.

The next morning, the shaman left the village and went to a place in the forest where he knew the warriors would be. It was a small valley with an entrance at each end. No stream flowed through the valley so it was not easy to find. It was located between two high cliffs, which made it difficult to enter except by the way of hidden trails located at each end of the valley.

The shaman entered the valley late at night so that the darkness hid him from view. Guards standing by the trail did not see him as he walked noiselessly by. He went straight to the camp and sat beside the fire pit without being observed by anyone. He remained there all night. When the warriors awoke in the morning they were surprised, but not concerned, when they found him.

They gathered around him and waited for him to speak because they had great respect for him and in fact even feared him. He looked at them in a kindly manner and said they should eat their first meal of the day. Food was brought to him, and they all ate glancing at him nervously. When they had finished, water was brought in a bowl and the shaman washed his face and hands. He thanked them for their courtesy and asked that all should be present. Some forty young men surrounded him as he talked.

"Why do you put your village in danger by your actions?" he asked. "Do you know that you have caused great concern in your village, and the chief and council are displeased with you?"

There was shuffling of feet and an embarrassed silence until two young men, apparently the leaders, stepped forward.

"Oh, Great One, we are angry that the white men have settled in a valley that we consider to be sacred, for it was there that our ancestors first lived and are buried. We ask that you give us your blessings to go and remove these people from the land of our ancestors."

The shaman sat in silence for some time before he answered the young men.

"I find it strange that you did not consult your chief or council before you decided to take this action and now you ask me to bless your foolishness. You have shown little responsibility for your actions or their aftermath. Have you thought that perhaps your leaders would prefer to ask the white people if they would leave this valley, to tell them why we considered it sacred?

"*Do you think that violence toward other men is the only way to solve a problem? You have shown disrespect for our ways. I will never bless ignorant actions by ignorant people. But, I realize you are young and unknowledgeable about the ways of nature and the Great Spirit.*

"*I have been told by a power greater than you shall ever know to intercede on your behalf with the white people and they will go to another valley. I promise. Now return to your village and ask forgiveness for your foolishness.*"

The shaman rose and left them standing, staring at his receding figure. It seemed to disappear into the forest before they could move or speak. Each looked at the other and knew they must obey this remarkable man. Who else could have found this place? Who else could walk into their guarded camp and sit by their fire pit unnoticed until daylight?

As he walked along an unseen trail, the shaman thought of the young men and was worried because this was just one of the many instances that would be sure to occur regarding native land and the white people. His heart was heavy within him for his people.

He knew what the future was going to bring and tears welled up in his eyes. Knowing the future made everything seem futile. Why bother when all is lost? He stopped this line of thought and felt blessed that he could perhaps heal wounds and stop the pain for now.

For two days he walked and finally came to the valley in question. He walked straight into the white people's midst and sat by a fire in front of a small structure that, by its appearance, had been hurriedly built. The white people looked at him in amazement. He was tall, with greying hair and braids that fell past his shoulders. His back was straight and he had a regal bearing. He wore leather pants with moccasins and no shirt. A leather necklace with a beaded circle hung on his chest. In his hand he carried an eagle feather.

A woman entered the structure, then two men emerged. One of the men was a priest and the other was obviously some kind of leader. They walked to the fire pit, and the priest said, "Who are you that you come into our village and sit by my fire pit without being invited?"

Looking straight ahead, the shaman answered, "I am the shaman of the tribe that lives on the land that you occupy. Who are you that comes here and claims this land as though it were yours?"

The white man made as if to answer, but the priest held up his hand to silence him and the man left. The priest studied this shaman and came to the conclusion that despite their greetings, perhaps they could talk this problem over. In any event, he wanted to hear what this obviously important man had to say.

"Perhaps I have not been a good host and I apologize for the comments made," he said. "Could I offer some drink or food since you have come a long way?"

"I will be pleased to drink with you and maybe I should not have been too hasty in my answer," replied the shaman. "Let us talk as brothers, both serving the Great Spirit as we do."

"I cannot agree that we serve the same god," said the priest. "You do not have the great cathedrals and churches that we have dedicated to our Father and where we worship Him."

"You are mistaken, my friend," said the shaman. "The world that the Great Spirit created is our cathedral and this is where we worship him. Besides, every man and woman is a walking church with our Lord within us. We need not tithe or pay for any service that the Great Spirit gives us. Our responsibility is to protect and care for our world and all that is in it. We believe every living thing is a part of the Great Spirit and must be treated with respect."

"I suppose we each have many things to learn of our different ways and beliefs," said the priest. "Let us discuss why you have come into our village."

"I have come here because you and your people have settled in a valley my people consider to be sacred," the shaman said. "Our ancestors first settled in this valley when they arrived here in the distant past and they are buried in this sacred ground."

The priest sat silent for a moment and then said, "We were not aware that anyone had lived here in the past, and I am filled with regret that we have offended your people. The people with me have lived in very poor conditions in a place over the sea where they have come from. There was no chance there that they would ever own their own land and be able to support themselves comfortably. They hoped to have a new life here for themselves and their families. Never did they want to disturb your people and take what is yours."

The shaman reflected on what the priest had said and replied, "I believe what you have told me and my people will not harm you. Our young warriors were prepared to drive you from the area, but the wisdom of our chief and council dissuaded them.

"I have been instructed by them to offer you a better valley to settle in that is not far from this one. It has water and all the things you will require. Our people will not bother you there and will do what we can to help you."

The priest showed his surprise at the generosity of the natives and thanked the shaman. He said he would consult with his people and asked the shaman to eat and rest while he did this. Later, the priest, accompanied by several men, returned to the shaman and said they all agreed they would be happy to accept the offer of a different valley and wanted to thank the chief and council for being so generous and forgiving of their trespass.

As dusk was approaching, the shaman told his hosts that he must return to his village as soon as possible and said goodbye to the white men. He rose and seemed to disappear as quickly as he had appeared.

Two days later, the people of the valley were surprised to see the shaman sitting quietly in front of his lodge. The chief and council were informed that he had returned and so made haste to go to his lodge to see him. When they had assembled, he told them all what had occurred between him and the white men. They felt that he had done well and agreed with what he had arranged.

In the days that followed, many of the people of the village went to see the white people. The young men even helped them move and settle in the new valley. Friendships were made and the two groups learned from each other. The shaman had several visits from the priest. It was said that the priest enjoyed their discussions so much that eventually he gained a different perspective about the native religion and accepted it as he did his own in some respects.

BORN MANY TIMES

2. BORN MANY TIMES

Born Many Times was a famous shaman of the Onandaga tribe, part of the Iroquois Confederacy. He lived in a trying time for all the natives in the New World. The white men were arriving in such large numbers that the native people were concerned for their own survival.

The white men brought their diseases, which had been unknown to the natives, and the tribes' numbers were being decimated. With their greed for land, broken promises, lies, and lack of respect for the native culture, there was constant trouble. Through all this, Born Many Times had to try and assure his people that they would survive to save their culture.

Born Many Times was not his real name. He had been born to an older man and his young woman. The name he received at birth was never mentioned again after he was given this new name when he was ceremonially raised to manhood. During his early youth he developed a keen sense of nature and came to understand the life of plants and how they could serve mankind. Because of this he was placed for further training with the medicine woman of his tribe.

During this period of his life he began to have visions of other lives that he had previously lived. He was not prepared for this information and discussed it with the tribal shaman, with whom he had developed a close relationship.

With the help of the shaman, he explored these insights more thoroughly. He was amazed to find that they became more acceptable to him as he explored them, and in time they became part of his existence as a native.

Soon the medicine woman and the shaman began to consult with Born Many Times about problems that he could solve with seeming great ease although they had found themselves hopelessly beyond their depth. Many of the things he said made them think he had made contact with the Great Spirit, but he took great pains to tell them that what he learned was available to everyone.

About this time, the young shaman decided he must find solitude within the forest so he could meditate in seclusion and without disturbance. As his fame had spread, so many people were coming to him for help that he could not find time to be alone. Seekers came not only from his own tribe. Every tribe in the Iroquois Nation was now clamoring for his time.

Born Many Times went deep into the forest and built a lodge to live in beside a small clear pond. People who did find him were surprised at the simple way he lived: they could see no food and wondered how he survived. Strangely, though, after they left his presence they would forget all about him and could not describe the place where he lived.

It was about this time that he made an appearance to Two Faces, about whom I have written a book, and so became visible to me as I consulted with the spirit of Two Faces. He appeared in a mysterious way and left in the same manner. He was unobtrusive during the time he had lived with this tribe and in fact always remained a mysterious figure.

This memorable man would not stay long in one place. His reason, as he explained it, was because there was so much to do and so little time available in one lifetime. One wonders how he could become so well-known and respected without the modern communication that we enjoy in our time and space.

It became evident to those who knew him that he could not have obtained all his knowledge without help from somewhere beyond the usual means. Many times he would hint as to the source of his information, but the people could not understand the importance of what he said. This went on for many years until finally a meeting was arranged by the chiefs and shamans of most of the Iroquois tribes to find out once and for all what they could learn from Born Many Times. This would give everyone the chance to satisfy his or her curiosity about this man and separate facts from fantasy.

They decided to hold the meeting in a large open field with a stream running through it. On one side there was a small hill where the chiefs and councils would sit. It was situated just below a ridge so Born Many Times could stand above them and the rest of those gathered. In this way everyone could hear and see him easily.

On the morning of the pre-arranged day the people gathered, holding ceremonies and renewing old acquaintances. So many were in attendance that special arrangements had to be made in order to accommodate them all. Born Many Times was not among them and some wondered if he had changed his mind about coming. But the chiefs assured them that he would be there at the appointed time.

After a small meal and refreshments the people gathered below the hill and the chiefs and councils took their places and waited patiently for Born Many Times to appear.

And appear he did in his usual, unusual way. He walked among the people quite unobtrusively not speaking to anyone.

In fact most people did not even notice him.

He was not wearing feathers, bones, and beads as most of the shamans did. He was bare to the waist, wearing pants and moccasins. His hair was combed straight back with braids falling on each side of his head. He was dressed as most men there were, with the exception of the chiefs.

Born Many Times walked slowly to the hilltop, stopping to greet the chiefs, councils, and other shamans that were known to him. He appeared so natural to the people that they wondered what was so special about him. But to those who knew him, his appearance was only part of this special man.

He stood tall on the hilltop and looked at the assembled people. He felt their pain and frustration. It was so familiar to him. If he could only give them what they expected, but he knew this was impossible. The future, as he knew it, left no alternatives.

One of the best-known chiefs of the Confederacy stood and spoke to him. "We, the chiefs and councils, welcome you and want you to know that we respect your willingness to be here. This is not an inquisition, but a desire to better know you and your good works among us."

The people cheered his words, and another chief stood and said, "You are favored among our people and many stories about you and your deeds are told around the campfires of our tribes. We do not doubt the truth of these stories, but some claims made are beyond belief. We want to dispel any lies and seek the truth."

There was voiced agreement from the people as Born Many Times stood and faced them. "I am pleased to be here and will try to answer the questions you have. I have done nothing more than what other shamans have done. They work through the Great Spirit on your behalf as I do."

As the second chief sat down another chief rose and said, "Recently you were in my village when young warriors were about to attack white people who were settling in a sacred valley of our tribe. You stopped the foolish warriors and negotiated with the white people to settle in another valley. I ask how you did this and how did you know they would accept another valley as you told the warriors they would?"

Born Many Times replied, "My chief, it was just logic and common sense. The white people did what they did in ignorance of the value of the sacred valley to your people. Your warriors were reacting as young people have always reacted when challenged. In the future we will have to learn to negotiate with the white people, because there are now too many to ignore. But I say to you, they cannot be trusted to keep their word."

This last statement was a shock to the people and they felt a fear they had never experienced before. Another chief stood and asked, "By your words and past deeds I want to know this: can you see the past and the future?"

Born Many Times said, "I can see the past because I have lived in it as you have done. I can unfortunately see the future also, but I will not divulge it, because no man should know the future."

The astounded look on everyone's faces told Born Many Times that he had perhaps gone too far. A chief stood and said, "I have never seen you before in my life and you do not know me so if you can do as you say, tell me who I am and who my tribe is."

Born Many Times looked at the man and realized he was backed into a corner and could do nothing but answer the man. "You are a chief of a small tribe of the Cayuga and live in a village close to the Oswega. Your woman is of the Oswega tribe and you have three boys and one girl. You have recently made an alliance with another tribe called the Wenro and hope your son will marry the daughter of one of their chiefs."

The chief, who was still standing, was astonished by the things Born Many Times told him. "You are correct in all you said, but I want you to tell me what the future is for me and my family."

Born Many Times, still standing, said, "This I will never do for individuals. I have not come here to play games with my ability, nor to waste it. You know full well who you are and the future is for you to decide, not me."

Born Many Times faced the people and said, "I have told you that I will not read the future, but I will in just this instance. Our people will suffer greatly.

"The white men are coming in ever greater numbers and there is no way to stop them. Many battles will be fought by our warriors, but to no avail because it will not stop what will be. Disease and misery will be our lot for the next two hundred years and then we will begin to assert our rights among sympathetic white leaders. I will speak no more."

He turned abruptly and disappeared down the opposite side of the hill away from the people. They were bewildered by what they had heard and there was a mixture of anger and fear in their faces. The leading chief rose and tried to calm their fears. "Do not fear the future," he said. "We will continue to negotiate with the white people when necessary and if we do it in good faith, surely the white people will do likewise."

Some of the people were heartened by what the chief said but most realized, because of past events, that his words were hollow. Many had lost relatives and friends due to the white man's sickness and they knew past agreements had not been kept by the white people.

It was quite a while after this that I came in contact with Born Many Times. He had approached Two Faces, whose life story I was writing. Two Faces was concerned as to where his loyalties lay because he was half-white and half-native. Born Many Times told him that his heart was native but his mind was white, and he had to live by that.

3. THE JOURNEY BEGINS

Perhaps I need to explain that I am an intuitive person who has developed the ability to see scenes from the past when I wish to, to communicate with persons who are no longer in body and to hear and see their life stories as they unfold.

The first person I wrote about, Red Snake, appeared to me when I was on an Indian site with my friend, archaeologist Dr. Norman Emerson, with whom I was working when I decided to "come out of the closet," so to speak, about my ability. Red Snake later came to me and told and showed me his life story. As a result, I wrote a book bearing his name (Red Snake, 1993: Hampton Roads Publishing Company, Inc.)

I then wrote the story of Red Snake's grandson, Running Bear (Running Bear, 1996: Hampton Roads Publishing Company, Inc.), and of Running Bear's stepchild, Two Faces (Two Faces, 1997: Hampton Roads Publishing Company, Inc.) It was when I was hearing and seeing Two Faces's story that Born Many Times came into Two Faces's life, and so into mine.

I could not erase from my mind my encounter with this strange person, who appeared out of nowhere to speak to Two Faces. I spent much effort to try to locate him again. Finally, contact was made through my spirit helpers, and Born Many Times agreed to speak to me and gave me permission to quote him in this story. I have hesitated for many months, knowing that the material to be presented would infringe on many people's belief systems and is contrary to certain currently-accepted knowledge and historical data.

However, through the insistence of friends and family, I present the following as it has been told to me by Born Many Times. Please remember these are not my own beliefs or knowledge but what has been given to me by this remarkable person who is no longer in a body but comes to me as a spirit. I cannot deny his statements, nor do I dismiss them. I was brought up in a Christian family and raised in a society that taught that the things learned in school were true and factual. I was also taught that the church and the royal family were supreme in the British Empire, as it was known in my early days.

So with this background I present the following:

Born Many Times was taller than one would expect, with dark eyes and a lean, muscular figure. He made no pretenses of friendliness, but neither was he rude or offensive. You could easily tell he was not one given to many excesses. His clothes were not outstanding and he appeared as an ordinary native.

The first thing he asked me was, "Do you believe in reincarnation? Because if you do not, I will be wasting my time."

My answer was in the affirmative because I had never felt one life was sufficient to learn all that one needed to learn.

"I will return to places in history that I have lived in and know the truth of, because there are so many misconceptions in your present about these times.

"I know you personally have a strong interest in Alexander the Great and that you do not believe what you have been told about this man."

He could not have surprised me more; I have always had a special interest in this man. I wondered how he knew how I felt. He began:

I was once a younger cousin to Philip, the father of Alexander, and I was made companion to him by his father. My name was Adonis and I had served in Philip's army most of my life. I was twenty-three, just a few years older than he, when asked to be Alex's companion. First, you must be aware that we lived very differently than you do today. Ours was a military order. We were constantly surrounded by enemies, and at an early age we had to learn to defend ourselves.

The kingdom of Macedonia was fairly secure because we had developed good fighting skills from years of combat.

Alexander and Aristotle

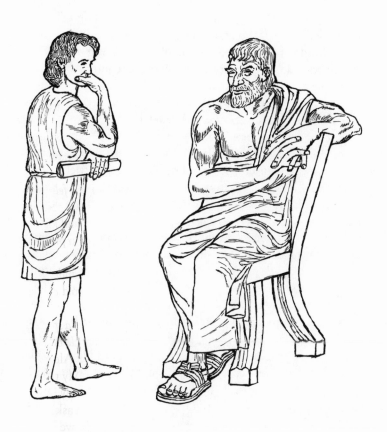

We had no war machines as you have now. Our most important asset was the powerful horses that we rode into combat. This, along with our skill with the sword and lance, made the difference.

Alex was a superb horseman from the time he first sat on a horse at the age of three. Most of our growing-up time was spent learning about our history and the different parts of our world where we lived. This was followed by studying different languages and some of the literature. Alexander could speak and read six different languages and could understand and make himself understood in several more. We were required to attend all the plays at the many theaters in our capital.

Long hours were spent with philosophers who taught us our religious beliefs and rules of social behavior.

Not that Alex worried about social behavior. As the son of the monarch he would one day be the leader, so he had plenty of freedom. In your day he would be like a spoiled, rich man's child. Women were always available, and contrary to what some people think, he was interested in women, not men, and his sexual appetite was very strong.

It must be understood that the state was controlled by one man and his kin. There was no end of men able and willing to teach Alex everything he needed to know about riding, fighting and all the skills and strategies he would need in warfare. Most of these men were relatives of the monarch and held powerful posts in the ruling group of our country. The monarch's power was absolute. He kept a strong hand on all matters of state.

As Alex grew older, he was given more responsibility, which he accepted without complaint. His mother and sisters gave him all the support he needed. He was mild in manner but could become angry if he thought you were doing wrong. He was careful to keep on good terms with the people who counted. Many thought he was rather feminine in his ways, but they soon learned he could be the opposite when it counted.

His horsemanship was better than most, and his swordsmanship was excellent. He practiced every day with the best of the country's swordsmen. He was not especially good with bow and arrow but could hold his own with the lance. Of course it was well known that not many could best him in horsemanship. His horse was the envy of those who knew him.

Not all his time was spent on war exercises. He enjoyed plays and banquets with his family and friends. He was very partial to his family and his relatives. His mother and sisters were the joy of his life, and he doted on them.

Everyone considered him to be a very kind and considerate person. Alexander's father assigned Aristotle to educate Alex so he had the best teacher his time had to offer. As his companion, I was included in these lessons and was grateful that I could learn from such a great teacher.

During his teenage years, the adjoining countries around Macedonia had been defeated in warfare by his father, who now controlled the trading routes of grain and commodities at that time. During his father's absence, Alex had to take his place in matters of state. One of these matters was a delegation from a country to their east that was making demands on them. Alex kept them pacified until his father returned, but his father, not being as obliging as Alex, made hostile threats to them.

They returned to their homeland, which was called Persia, and began to make threatening forays against the Macedonians. Philip had made plans to attack the countries to their east, but before he could carry them out he was murdered. Alexander then became ruler in his place, and from the beginning he made sure he was the only ruler in the area.

After all was settled in his own country, he recruited an army sufficient for his purpose and went to meet the threat of Persia, conquering as he went. His army shared the spoils of war, and they were many.

Finally he faced Darius of Persia who was the most dangerous of his enemies. Alexander's country had been attacked many years previously by the Persians and they had not forgotten it.

In those days, the army generals and leaders would take their families with them when they fought. They would stand on a hilltop away from the actual battleground and issue orders from this comparatively safe place. Alexander was the exception to this. He rode his horse and fought alongside his generals and men.

All his methods of warfare were different from those expected by his enemies. This is what made him so successful. Besides being in the field with his men, he divided them into separate groups making it possible to fight in more than one place at a time instead of being congregated together and so an easy target. This confused his enemies because they did not know how to fight this way.

Because of this, he won quite easily with a minimal loss of men. Another thing he did was to send a group on horseback around the opposing army to take captive the leaders and generals that were on the hilltop. This would then take them away from being in control of the battle. But Darius and his staff saw what was happening and took to their horses, running away, leaving his wife, daughters and attendants to the mercy of Alexander.

They were taken captive, but by orders from Alexander they were treated as honored guests and were not harmed. He met and talked with them in person and told them he was not their conqueror but their protector. His men and I were surprised by this because this was not the way most victors had behaved from time immemorial.

The women of Darius could hardly believe this was happening. They expected to be raped and abused as the spoils of war. They were certainly grateful for what Alexander did. He kept his word, and they were treated as royal guests.

Alexander and his army continued on, conquering all in their path. They wasted considerable time with a place surrounded by water that was difficult to attack. Whenever he was attacking a city it was given a chance to surrender, but if it did not, he put many of the people to death for resisting.

After some time and many battles, Alexander was again confronted by Darius and the Persians. He defeated them, but Darius and his generals again fled. But Alexander was not about to give up and he pursued them. Days later, he was approached by Darius's generals who gave him Darius's head. He inquired as to what had happened, and they told him they had executed Darius because they thought Alexander would spare them if they killed his enemy. Alexander was furious and had all the generals executed because he had planned to take Darius alive, as he had promised his wife.

Another time, when they had taken the great Persian city of Persopolis, his generals got drunk and burned and looted the city. Again Alexander was furious and had many of his men punished for this outrage. While there he met a young Jewish girl whom he later married.

This was an unexpected event and I am sure Alex had not seen this in his future. However, I knew from experience that he did have an interest in women and was quite active sexually.

This girl appeared one morning at the camp where Alex was meeting with some people from the city of Persopolis.

There was a commotion among the guards and Alex wanted to know what the problem was. A young girl was brought before him, and without any regard for her safety she began to berate him and the people gathered. The guards made to silence her, and Alex bade them to let the girl continue.

She was very angry that her people were not included in the discussions that were going on and wanted them to be heard. Alex asked why her people were not invited to attend the meeting. He was told that they were not Persians or permanent residents of the country. They were Jewish technicians and artisans who were hired by Darius to do the work on the palace.

Unlike the countries around them, the Persians went to great trouble to hire and pay for the builders needed to build the great palaces that were in Persia, not like Egypt, where the laborers were slaves taken for this work and never paid.

Alex asked the girl to speak and explain why she wanted to address him. She said her countrymen had been hired to do the work in Persopolis and now they wanted to be paid and allowed to return to their homeland. The Persians said that since most of their work had been destroyed by our men, they felt it was not their obligation to pay them and wanted them to stay and do the work on repairs to the building.

Alexander grew angry and told the Persians they were to pay the Jewish people and all the other technicians they had recruited and let them return to their respective homelands.

In the days following, Alexander's orders were carried out under the scrutiny of the girl and others. During this time Alexander became very infatuated with the girl. She was slim and of average height, very pretty and charming.

The result was that Alex married the girl, and I can say that he remained in love with her until his death. He also permitted all the administrators and government of Persia to stay in place, but left a small tribunal of his men to oversee them.

Alexander spared the royal family of Darius, but the concubines were given to his men to use as they pleased. It has been noted that Darius had more than one hundred children by his concubines. The children were spared from harm and their mothers were given their freedom after his men left.

Many of his men began to grumble about what they perceived to be Alexander's lenient treatment of his enemies, but after many long conversations with me and the other generals, they could understand his feelings.

He told us, "Many hundreds of years have been taken to build the cultures and forms of government these enemies have. It has also taken many centuries to build the beautiful buildings these cultures have erected. Would it not be a shame to destroy these things that have taken so long to develop just because the people act and do things differently than what we do?

"The gold, silver, money and other treasures, and the food we need we take and divide. But the greatest treasure we leave them. These are the things that they have taken centuries to create and accumulate. These are their greatest treasures.

"Whenever they have leaders that abuse them and treat them badly we will replace them with our own people. But those who have governed wisely should be left in place. In this manner we need to leave only a few people to oversee them.

"Otherwise we would have to waste good soldiers to leave

as administrators and would weaken ourselves for future combat. This we cannot afford to do. One good man left to administer is better than a hundred soldiers if the people appreciate what you do for them."

After this, everyone understood his wisdom. After taking several cities on the way, we eventually arrived in Egypt. There were two reasons that Alexander wanted to take Egypt. The first was that this was the country his mother had been born in, and the second was the need for the food that Egypt produced in such abundance. He knew his army must be fed while on their expedition. Here he encountered little difficulty because the Egyptians had heard by then that we were coming and had decided not to put up a fight.

We made our headquarters in a small fishing village on the ocean shore. Alexander drew in the sand a plan for a city that he wanted to be built here in his honor. It was to be called Alexandria. He would leave his cousin Ptolemy in charge of this country and Ptolemy was to build the city. It was just a small fishing village at the time, but Alexander could see the possibility of a great port and a trading center and he realized its potential future economic value.

While he was in this area, Alexander decided he would go to see the great Sorceress of Ammon. He had a question to ask her. This meant a difficult ride across the desert, but it made no difference to him because he felt he had to go.

One morning, we left with ten soldiers and four Egyptian guides. Some of us were on Arabian horses more suitable than our own to the desert, and we took ten camels loaded with guides and gear.

It seemed to be an eternity before we reached a small tent compound where the oracle lived. Sand, sun, and flies tormented us on the trip. We were given a tent in which to rest and eat before Alexander was to see the oracle. Servants brought us fruit and water. We wondered where they found the water and fruit in this terrible isolated little place.

A servant came and beckoned Alexander to accompany him and he motioned for me to come, too. We entered a tent not much bigger than the one given us. A huge rug covered the floor and cushions were spread everywhere. On a pile of cushions sat a woman with her face hidden behind a silk scarf. No part of her showed but we knew she was old by her voice. Her eyes peered out at us like black holes.

A servant told us to sit on the cushions in front of her. It was indicated that I was to sit back away from both of them. The woman's voice was hardly audible to me, and I wondered if Alexander could hear her. She asked why we had come. Alexander told her we had come so he could ask a question of her. She told him to ask. He hesitated a moment then asked, "Can you see the future and if so what is there for me?"

We sat quietly in front of her and though we could not see her plainly we knew that she was observing and assessing us. She was motionless for such a long time I began to feel uncomfortable. Suddenly, she began to talk in a quiet voice that penetrated one's senses.

"So, you are the great leader of the Macedonians who has been busy conquering all the countries to your south. Let me ask you a question. Why? At first it was to protect yourselves from the Persians, but you accomplished this. So why do you continue? Have you become bloodthirsty and wish to kill and torment others? Or are you on a quest to prove to the world that you are the greatest leader and soldier? Answer me this."

Alexander was silent for a moment, and I could tell that he was uncomfortable. "I am not what it appears to you that I am. I feel that I am not seeking to be the best, but only to help those that need help. From the time I was born I was taught to fight and be a warrior. But I was also taught to love those things that have beauty and to respect culture. Too long has mankind in most countries been abused by their leaders. I have tried to make these people realize that to have good government they must have good leaders.

"Every country I have conquered so far has had the leadership changed to bring this about. I have not taken their women or treasures for myself. I realize my men have, but they must be paid for their services. That is why I am in your country, because those under our rule must also be fed. Your country has food to spare. It has been governed by corrupt officials who must be replaced. I try to keep the loss of life to a minimum, but I know this is not always possible and it grieves me.

"To give one's life is a terrible cost to pay. But if one pays this price as the cost of an honorable ideal then perhaps it is worth the price. I have not asked one of my men to do what I would not do myself.

"They know why we are engaged in this campaign and they agree with it and my leadership. There is not one man among us who is not known to me. I grew up with every one of them and they know I consider each one to be my friend.

"When I inherited my position from my father there was a great responsibly placed on my shoulders. I was honor-bound and respectful of my father's wishes to complete the things that he had begun. Therefore, I had no choice but go to war against the Persians. While planning this expedition I had many choices to make. The most important was who was to accompany me. Were they the ones who were most loyal to me or the ones who were not?

"I made the decision to take those who were not. I considered it better to have enemies I could see and control than those whom I could not. After we had been successful in our battle against the Persians, I left in charge those whom I considered to be poor soldiers but good administrators. I have followed this procedure after every successful encounter. After finding the Persians so corrupt in high places within this country I decided to continue in my endeavor to eliminate corruption everywhere I went. That is why I am where I am and I intend to continue.

There was a long silence and we wondered if she had fallen asleep. "We are all special," she said at last, "But some have different destinies than others. Yours is to expand the boundaries of your country and leave the world a better place than you found it. This is very commendable but you know it will only last as long as you do. The serpent called corruption merely lies buried in the sand until you have passed and then it will rear its ugly head again, strong as ever.

"You were nineteen when you became king of your country, but you had the ability needed to put you where you are now. I can see that those who are your kin will be your undoing and that greed will follow your accomplishments.

"Only history will give you the honor you will deserve. You have given the world much, but it will not be known until centuries after you have left this life. Your kindness to your enemies will always be remembered by them and will be repeated by others long after you have gone. What will be, will be, my son."

Again there was a long silence and the servant motioned for us to leave. In our own tent, Alexander was disturbed but said nothing. He knew he had found out what he wanted to know and did not like what he had heard. For myself, I had little faith in what she had said, which to me now is a strange thing. I should have known this woman could see the future, but did not. I now knew more about Alexander than I had known before and felt proud to have served such a courageous man.

The next day we returned to where Alexandria was to be, again enduring the blazing sun, heat and insects. Alexander began planning our next program immediately. He and his generals decided that they would continue to the east. Leaving our women in Alexandria with Ptolemy, we departed.

Alex had discussed whom he should leave to build the Alexandria he wanted. There were several men who would want the challenge and Alex carefully investigated each one. When he made his choice of Ptolemy, I was surprised and said so.

He laughed and told me he wanted to remove Ptolemy from the hazardous work of warfare because he was not a good soldier. But he was a good administrator, knew geography and astronomy, and knew how to obey orders, and, most important, Ptolemy was faithful to him. He had been the one most angry when the army had destroyed Persopolis. Alexander had been angry, too, but realized the soldiers had only done what they had because they were the conquerors. They felt this gave them the right to plunder what they had won. This type of barbarism is caused by the stress of warfare.

During the next seven years, Alexander covered great distances and managed what had never before been accomplished by other men. He overran and conquered many countries, always leaving each one a better place by replacing its government with more patient and caring people. During this time many of his own men rebelled, but he was always able to straighten out the problems amongst them.

The main complaint was their long absence from home. Many of his soldiers wanted to return to their families. It became apparent that many of his officers objected to Alexander's practice of letting former enemies and those they had previously conquered get favored positions in his army. In particular, he had let Persian army personnel join in the campaign. These and other former enemies now held positions of authority.

I spoke to Alexander about this problem many times, but he still persisted. He told me that he could use the best these people had to offer, and that this was a way to get the confidence of the conquered people. Eventually he had to listen to his men, and he decided at last to go back home.

But, unfortunately, he became ill in Babylon and this delayed his return. So much so, that a few of his officers decided that the only way they would be able to leave was to hasten his death, which they felt was imminent anyway.

There were other reasons they decided to do this. One was that they wanted a bigger share of what had been captured, and they did not want to share the spoils with anyone who had not been part of their army from the beginning. Secretly they began to slowly poison Alexander and withhold medical treatment. And so he died.

Immediately upon Alexander's death, the officers began to squabble among themselves as to how to divide the territory they had garnered over the years. No one wanted the responsibility of returning Alexander to his homeland. His body was treated with respect, only because his soldiers demanded that it should be. Word was sent to their homeland telling about his death, but it was many weeks before the news was received. There was no way to send information except by messenger.

When Ptolemy heard the news, he immediately dispatched Egyptian envoys to claim the body if possible. He included people with the knowledge of mummification and ordered it to be transported safely to Egypt. When they finally arrived with the body, it had decomposed a good deal because it could not last long in the hot weather. It had been embalmed by Babylonian standards, but what they had used was not a lasting preservative.

The generals agreed that Alexander's body could go to Egypt and they released it with some relief. When it arrived in Egypt, there was no tomb ready in which to display it, so it was stored in a building in Thebes until one could be built in Alexandria.

Alexander had three wives. His first and favorite wife was the Jewish girl he had married in Persopolis. He had married the other two for convenience to cement alliances. His Jewish wife had stayed in Alexandria with Ptolemy. She had been successful in establishing a Jewish section in the city and a graveyard for her people.

Ptolemy had gone ahead and built the city as planned by Alexander. It was rectangular in shape with a surrounding wall. A port had been constructed and the famous lighthouse, one of the seven wonders of the world, completed. It towered above an island in front of the harbor. Its light, which was reflected off a large brass dish, could be seen for miles out to sea. Alexandria had become a thriving port city with large wide roadways and exceptionably good port facilities.

The Nile river was the roadway of Egypt. Boats plied the waterway loaded with grain and farm produce. The Nile valley was very fertile and could produce three crops a year. This Egyptian produce was eagerly traded for in the busy port of Alexandria, and a large, cosmopolitan citizenship grew. There were boats from every region of the Mediterranean putting into the port.

As the city grew, it became prosperous enough for the Ptolemies through the ages to build a large library, second to none in the world. They built reservoirs and large underground water systems. The government buildings were tremendous structures. It was luxury living at its finest for that time.

Since the Egyptians worshiped many animal gods, Ptolemy began the worship of the bull. In one area he had a stable built for the bulls. Under this stable there were tunnels dug on many levels with little alcoves along the side. A man would run into the tunnel and the bulls were sent in. It was pitch dark in the tunnel and the man had no way to avoid the bull unless he could step into an alcove until the bull ran by. Naturally many men did not make it, but the bulls always did. Why men did this was probably to show their bravery, but it was a really stupid practice.

When the tomb was finally ready, the body of Alexander was brought from Thebes. It had deteriorated badly. It had been wrapped in a purple robe which had deteriorated in the damp storage area and his clothes had bled their dye onto his bones. His face had been attacked by rats and other rodents and was in very poor shape. By then Alexander had been dead for more than two years. At no time was his sarcophagus made of gold, as has been reported. His surviving generals had a better use for this metal and felt it was foolish to waste it in this manner. To say it was gold and was stolen on the way to Egypt is nonsense. Nor was his sarcophagus in Alexandria made of crystal. It was stone, like those of all the pharaohs.

But nowhere in the world were there better craftsmen who could restore a dead body to its original appearance than in Egypt. With wax and plaster they rebuilt the body of Alexander so that when he was dressed in his uniform he looked as he had when alive. He was placed in the tomb that had been built in the Jewish graveyard, as his wife had asked.

What is left of this tomb is under the Nebi Daniel mosque in Alexandria. It is about thirty feet down under the washroom of the present-day mosque. It is known historically that the Jewish graveyard was here.

Later, after Cleopatra and Antony had been killed, their Roman conqueror visited the tomb and said, "So this is the man who was the greatest general of all!" And, swinging his sword at the body of Alexander, he knocked off his nose. He regretted this action and had the wax nose replaced.

In about five A.D., the government of Greece was asked if they wanted the bones of Alexander as well as his sarcophagus. The Eastern church objected as they had enough competition as it was and didn't want someone else whom the people might worship. They did decide to accept the sarcophagus. However the boat that was returning it to its homeland ran into trouble off the coast of Lebanon, and the sarcophagus is still in that country.

The bones of Alexander were sent to a Muslim monastery situated in the desert west of Alexandria and they remain there today. The brothers at this monastery will tell you that the bones were sent there from Alexandria in the fifth century but they were told only that they were the bones of an important person. These bones have been seen by some people during the last few years. They were stained a bluish-purple color.

4. CLEOPATRA, QUEEN OF THE NILE

*At another time, Born Many Times told me the story of Cleopa-
tra who, he said, has been wronged by supposedly historical information. He wanted the truth to be known about this remarkable
woman. His story of other lives he lived continues:*

In Cleopatra's lifetime, I was a priest and educator named
Appolludorus. Ptolemy, Cleopatra's father, gave me the task of
supervising her upbringing and seeing that she had the best his
kingdom had to offer. Historians do not know who the mother
of Cleopatra was. But I have been told her mother was a distant
cousin of Ptolemy, also named Cleopatra, and that Ptolemy had
fathered her.

Cleopatra was the thirteenth woman to be called by this
name since the time the first Ptolemy built Alexandria. Cleopatra and Alexander were popular names in those times. She
had a brother younger than herself, also born of Ptolemy, who
was a spoiled brat. Cleopatra was a difficult child, with a violent
temper, and she was very headstrong.

That is why I was chosen to educate and care for her. I must
admit I was not thrilled with the job but had no choice in the
matter. I had studied as a priest within the old religion of the
pharaohs but had changed to the new one popular with the new
Greek pharaohs called Ptolemy. The old religion still existed
but no longer had any authority.

The first Ptolemy pharaoh had built many outstanding
buildings in Alexandria and the next two leaders had carried

on with his wisdom and built Alexandria to be even more luxurious. Unfortunately after this the pharaohs deteriorated. Their palace became a place of intrigue and murder. The descendents of Ptolemy became obsessed with power and Egypt was soon corrupted.

When a ship entered the harbor of Alexandria, it was greeted by the sight of many buildings of splendor. There were the gymnasium, law courts, the forum, the library, the Ptolemie's tombs, the mausoleum of Alexander the Great, the museum, the royal palaces and many temples to different gods, along with other stately edifices.

These buildings were a blend of Egyptian and Greek architecture. Most of the cities that surrounded the Mediterranean had copied the architecture of the Egyptians in some way. Many engineers and architects of Egypt come to these countries to help with their building, and this was true in Greece.

Alexandria had become a cosmopolitan city. There were Greeks, Egyptians, Persians, Phoenicians, Latins, Armenians, Libyans, and people from the islands of Crete and Cyprus who brought with them different trades and contacts that added to the wealth of the city.

But despite all this, Cleopatra's father was part of the decline of Egypt. He mortgaged the wealth of Egypt to the Romans who helped him stay in power. This is the scene that Cleopatra was born into.

Eventually her father had me take her to Upper Egypt for her education, but I was well aware he just wanted to get her away from his palace because she was becoming more difficult to handle.

I recognized that Cleopatra was very intelligent and could learn quickly. She wanted to know everything there was to know. She had no patience with people who considered her to be a spoiled child of the pharaoh. She had less patience with men who tried to take advantage of her because she was female.

The day we left, the boats to take us up the Nile were piled high with her belongings. We made a stop at Thebes where, according to the custom of the time, she was deflowered, or lost her virginity. This was an Egyptian policy followed by the Greek leaders. Later, when I saw Cleopatra, she showed no signs of what she had been through and never mentioned it to me.

She was now thirteen years old and well developed physically. Rather tall for her age, she was well proportioned. She was not pretty, but was certainly attractive. Her most notable features were her eyes (which could look right through you) and the cultivated tone of her voice. She was quick to like or dislike a person. One had to be intelligent to warrant her attention, and as soon as she became bored with you she would dismiss you at once.

As we traveled up the Nile, we passed many towns and villages where the people came out to see Cleopatra. She was always charming and gracious with the poor of her country and did not talk down to them. This was a pleasant surprise to the people because they had always been treated with disdain by their Greek overlords.

This was to help her in her future relations with the people. She was the only Greek leader of Egypt who took the time to learn and speak Egyptian. She was also the only leader to understand and practice the Egyptian religion.

At the temples we visited, the priests were impressed with Cleopatra's intelligence and would talk with her for days on end. They gave her new insights about Egypt. She and I would spend long hours discussing what she had learned. Some of the people we met were from neighboring countries and she listened to their stories and added to her knowledge.

By the time we returned to Alexandria a year and a half later, Cleopatra was a changed person. No longer was she a vain, spoiled child. She now had more patience with people and had become a very clever politician. She listened to the people around her before giving an opinion. She especially encouraged the lower staff to confide in her and knew whom to cultivate as friends.

There was much intrigue in her father's palace, and it became necessary for him to go to Rome to get help. For this he had to borrow a large sum of money. In time he was made

Ptolemy XII. He died an alcoholic and was replaced on the throne by both Cleopatra and her young brother. Cleopatra was eighteen at the time and her brother was six.

This meant that her brother had regents to advise him. It was assumed that when he grew older he would marry Cleopatra, as was the custom of the rulers, and that eventually he would be the ruler.

But Cleopatra had other ideas. She detested this younger brother and the regents who controlled him. It was soon a divided camp. The intellectuals and academics, along with the Egyptian people, were behind Cleopatra, while the merchants and Greeks of Alexandria were behind her brother.

Cleopatra lived in Alexandria in a palace on the shore of the great harbor where all the royal quarters were situated. Hers was the last building beside a point of land on the east side. It was an impressive structure, being rather square in design with great columns on the side facing the water. There was a large, wide staircase leading down to the water's edge, and her royal barge was kept there. A large patio faced onto the water and this is where Cleopatra spent much of her free time. When she was not at home she was at the library reading and discussing philosophy with some of the greatest minds of her time. She could now speak eight or nine different languages and was, as I have said, the only Ptolemy to speak Egyptian.

Because of the power of the regents, Cleopatra did not have much say in the running of the government. She was constantly overruled in her decisions. But this was about to change. In Rome, Caesar Soter was contemplating an invasion of the countries to the east and he knew that Egypt still owed a considerable amount of money to his country. There was also a problem with Pompeii that he knew needed his attention. He therefore decided to annex Egypt, knowing it had a problem with leadership and was a weak target.

When he arrived in Alexandria, there was no resistance and he was kept isolated from Cleopatra by the regents and her brother. Cleopatra told me to bribe the guards and smuggle her into the palace wrapped in a rug as a present to Caesar.

He was at his desk at the time, signing the annexation papers to take over Egypt. He had found the regents to be conniving, dishonest people— especially the eunuch. You could imagine his surprise when the rug was unrolled and he saw the attractive young girl before his eyes.

Cleopatra was quick to explain why she had to be smuggled in to see him. After listening to Cleopatra, Caesar was furious with the regents and ordered their arrest immediately. Her younger brother was sent away from Alexandria. The regents were beheaded. Later the brother drowned while wearing his armor, which was not made of gold and had pulled him under the water. He was not a full pharaoh because he ruled only under the regents, and this is why his armor was not made of gold.

A few days later, the Egyptian army stormed Alexandria and Caesar was trapped on the point of land near Cleopatra's palace. He had to enter the water to save himself. He had on his full armor, but managed to swim to the palace where he took refuge with Cleopatra. Later he was able to get reinforcements from a harbor about twenty-five miles to the east and defeated the Egyptians.

Cleopatra was trying to convince Caesar not to annex her country. Finally an agreement was made. She was to finance his expedition to the east and supply part of Egypt's yearly crop to Rome. In time this would mean that Egypt supplied one quarter of Rome's food supply for the year. This still left enough for her people's needs.

Now that she was the sole ruler of Egypt, Cleopatra proved herself to be a shrewd and able administrator. The economy of Egypt became better than it had ever been before. Caesar gave her vast territories to manage. And, though the people of these other countries despised her, their economies improved with her help.

As is said historically, she and Caesar became lovers. But it was not a love match—it was merely sexual in nature. The custom among the pharaohs was to marry brother to sister in order to keep the bloodline untainted. They were merely following custom. Although they were not brother and sister, both were leaders of their countries. Cleopatra did bear children from their union but what was strange or immoral about that? After all, she was a woman. Most of the pharaohs had up to a hundred women as their concubines and most of these women bore children. It was only those with royal blood that had a brother-sister union.

Caesar returned to Rome with the younger sister of Cleopatra as a prisoner. She was paraded through the streets in chains and eventually executed as was their custom with a conquered enemy. Cleopatra did visit Rome, but only for a short time. She heard the rumors there that said she was a slut and could not be satisfied with one man. These were derived from jealousy and she paid them no attention. After all which woman in Rome was not a slut?

When she returned home Cleopatra worked hard to make Egypt a better place for her people. She did more than any other ruler to help her countrymen. She made herself available for all the religious ceremonies of the priests. She personally accompanied the bull god, Bacchus, on her royal barge for a special ceremony and this made a tremendous impression on her subjects. No pharaoh or leader in Egypt was better liked than Cleopatra was. Despite the fact that she was part of the hated Greeks that ruled them, she proved beyond a doubt by her actions that she was Egyptian first.

When Cleopatra went down the Nile on her royal barge, she dressed as Isis and the people loved it. To them she was the living god of love. Not only did she accept Isis and Osiris, but also Horus and Amon-Ra, and she celebrated the holy days and ceremonies with her people. She still continued her studies at the library, reading the great works of the philosophers and studying the maps of the world and the universe that were available there.

No ruler was ever better educated than she. Cleopatra could discuss philosophy with the most educated in the world at that time and was considered their equal. Her government was the best-managed Egypt ever had and the country grew richer because of it. These benefits were shared with her people in many ways. There was no poverty nor did people need to look for work.

About this time Caesar was murdered and Rome was now ruled by a triumvirate. This meant that there were three groups ruling Rome. It was made up of Octavius Caius, Marcus Antonius, and the senate. Octavius ruled the west and Antony ruled the east. Antony was known to Cleopatra because he had been to Egypt when she was a young girl and she remembered him.

Again, like Caesar, Antony felt that he should continue the war to the east to add to Rome's empire. And again to be able to do this he needed the funds necessary. Where better to get them than from Egypt? So he arrived in Alexandria and sent a message for Cleopatra to meet him.

When she received the message she realized that he was trying to make her feel that he was superior to her by not coming to her, but demanding that she go to him. If she had to go, she decided to make it an occasion to remember.

She had the royal barge decorated in all the luxury that Egypt had to offer. It was adorned with cloth of silver and gold. She was richly dressed to represent the goddess Isis.

On the day of her arrival, she had the people line the shoreline where she was to meet Antony. The people loved this display of Isis, and Antony was spellbound. Even in Rome he had never seen such luxury displayed.

Cleopatra was now in a dilemma. She had to do again what she had done with Caesar. One has to understand that in this time love and sex were not the same thing. So it meant that although Cleopatra did not love Caesar, she did engage in sex with him as was the custom in those days. Of course people of that time did not have sex with someone they disliked, but sex was not love.

When Cleopatra and Antony met they immediately liked each other, and later they did fall in love. But it must be remembered that Cleopatra was at first only trying to do the best she could for her country and was willing to sacrifice herself for that purpose. She truly thought by then that she was the living incarnation of Isis, who was the goddess of love.

As mentioned before, she was far from being a beautiful woman, but she had compelling eyes, strength of character, and a way of speaking that was more important than looks to discerning men. Needless to say Antony was most intrigued by her.

Despite what has been said, Cleopatra did not bankrupt her country and cause hardship by supplying Antony with what he needed to engage in warfare. In fact, her people were more prosperous than they had ever been under the other Ptolomies. It is true that the country suffered severe droughts at this time, but this was hardly the fault of Cleopatra. She made sure that all her people were well fed.

Antony was away most of the time, either in the field or in Rome. His relationship with Octavius became so strained that war between them was inevitable. So it came about that Antony was defeated by Octavius and, in complete despair, committed suicide. He died in Cleopatra's arms. It is said that she had decided to commit suicide, too, and chose to use the bite of a serpent to bring about her demise. This is completely false.

The story was told that, rather than drink poison, Cleopatra had chosen to die by the venom of a snake, as it was the emblem of Isis. It is said that she died by the bite of a viper, but this was not so. If indeed Cleopatra had chosen to die in this manner, she would have planned to use a cobra, not a viper. Cobra poison induces unconsciousness very quickly before death. The viper, however, leaves a victim in severe agony before death with the flesh badly blemished.

The story goes on to say that when Cleopatra's body was found, she had just two small marks on her arm, which rules out a viper. To secrete enough poison to kill an adult, a cobra would have had to have been at least four feet in length. It would require a basket of immense size in order to conceal a snake large enough to kill not just Cleopatra, but also her two attendants whose bodies were found with her.

Cleopatra and Mark Antony

History is not always recorded as truth. The account of Cleopatra's suicide by the use of a viper was the creation of Octavius in order to place Rome in a better light. It was pure propaganda. Cleopatra and her two maid servants died by decapitation. Soldiers of Octavius secretly entered the palace and wielded the swords which took their lives. Antony and Cleopatra were buried together as she had requested. Octavius now accomplished what Cleopatra had managed to avoid during her lifetime. Egypt was annexed by Rome.

Born Many Times is adamant that Cleopatra was one of the best leaders the world has had and feels it an injustice that she does not receive the credit she so greatly deserves. Whenever her name is mentioned, men tend to sneer or show contempt. Perhaps she is treated this way because she was a woman. If she had been a man she would have been venerated. Helen of Troy, Saint Joan of Arc, the Queen of Sheba, Golda Meier, Indira Ghandi, Eva Peron or Margaret Thatcher are all thought of in this way and why? They are all women leaders of our history. The world should be ashamed of the way history has treated this great leader, Cleopatra, Queen of Egypt.

5. IN THE BEGINNING

Born Many Times wanted to start his story by telling me what had happened to mankind in the distant past, so that I would understand what is to happen in the future. Both the past and the future made me uncomfortable. The past is cold and difficult to understand, and the future is unreliable to forecast.

So little is known or proven about past events. It was difficult for me to understand the environment that existed at the beginning of mankind's presence here and to conceive of all the problems that had to be coped with. The future is charged with what could happen and will, if certain things are not changed. But, then if they are changed, the future could also be different.

Born Many Times was not to be deterred from giving me this information, despite my reluctance to receive it. He told me, "There is no present history if you do not understand the past and future." So he began:

In the long ago man did live as we describe, a caveman's existence. In effect, he wandered and hunted for his food and took shelter where he could find it. His life was perilous because of the big animals living at that time. They were also hunters and he could easily be part of their meal. He and others like him lived every day in fear.

Because of his smaller size and inferior strength man realized that he needed help to defend himself against the stronger animals. Fortunately, he was gifted with more intelligence than they were and he soon devised ways to make it safer for himself.

He made tools from what was at hand to hunt with. The first was a sharpened wooden shaft which was quite effective. He had learned to make this shaft by observing the sharp thorns around him. He was continually being stuck with these sharp objects and decided to copy them.

He then learned to throw this shaft for greater effect. This proved to be effective, but he needed something sharp enough to penetrate the tough hide of most animals. Earlier, he had learned to use sharpened stones to cut up the animals he had killed. He learned that making the wooden shaft shorter and inserting a sharp stone in the end would make a better weapon. After this it was simple to make axes and other sharpened stone tools and weapons.

As his techniques improved, he learned that better weapons could be made. If the wooden shaft was shortened and feathers put on the end opposite the stone tip, he could propel the wooden shaft from a bow. Soon he had developed the bow and arrow. This became his main defensive and hunting tool for many years. He continued to use the spear for larger prey.

Now man had tools to hunt with which afforded him some protection. Unfortunately, he still lived in a transient manner while following the game he needed to hunt to survive. People lived together in small family units consisting, at the most, of fifteen people. This was the largest group that could safely stay mobile and hidden at the same time. The animals they hunted could only feed this number when the people were lucky enough to secure their prey. They gathered some vegetation to supplement their diet, but at this time it was mainly meat they lived on.

As time went on, they began to gather more food sources from vegetation. Eventually they started to practice farming in a primitive manner, but it was still difficult to survive. A large animal could wipe out half the family unit in a few moments and those that did survive had a hard time remaking a family unit again. If there were only a few people left, they would join another unit, if that was acceptable.

Later they began to make themselves permanent shelters and went into farming for some of their food. The women then tended the gardens and the men continued to hunt. As time went on and their tools became more proficient, it became easier to live without fear. Due to great environmental changes, sometimes catastrophic to all living things, even to themselves, some animals disappeared never to be seen again.

What has been described above happened to mankind many times and in many places, but always man has survived to start the same process over and over again. There were times he lasted longer periods before the next catastrophe occurred, and more intelligent progress was made each time. As man increased his knowledge, he increased his ability to survive.

As the Earth became more stable for his survival, man increased his living skills. Though most continued to hunt and gather there were those that chose to live in a larger community and farm for the greater part of their food source. They learned to store food for times they could not grow any. The men continued to hunt for meat, which they learned to store as well.

Animals were domesticated for meat and milk. Now that man had a good food source available and good shelter he created things that he needed in a more sophisticated manner. He also created a culture unique to his environment and eventually began to thank plants, animals or natural things for his survival, and slowly he began to worship these things. He then created replicas of these items to worship. In the beginning they were made of what was available nearby, such as wood, feathers, furs, stones, and shells.

In the meantime, there were other groups that did not farm but still existed in the old way, hunting and gathering. They became aware of the villages set up by their neighbors and began to be jealous of the other's comfortable style of living and their possessions. So it wasn't long before they started to attack these villages and steal away the objects they desired. The farm and village people had not supposed they would be attacked by their fellow humans and had not made provisions for their own security from this source.

They immediately began to fortify their villages with barricades either in a natural form or by building high fences. They also set about producing more efficient weapons with which to defend themselves. Thus, it was no longer animals that man feared, but man himself, and it has been this way ever since. Now mankind had entered a new phase of existence and jealousy had been invented.

Mankind had more than just humans to contend with. Nature in early times was very unpredictable. There were severe rainstorms and earthquakes that made their lives difficult. These things did make man's progress unreliable. Sometimes their work completed over centuries was obliterated in a matter of hours.

Mankind had many periods of cultural progress, some with technology more advanced than that of our present day. These were usually halted by Earth changes. Evidence being brought to light recently shows that some civilizations were further advanced than you are.

Earlier civilizations had a calendar more accurate than the Julian one, used by the Europeans until they found the New World and the natives there. These calendars were from cultures that had preceded the Europeans by thousands of years. They had accurate maps of your world unknown until the present time. Ancient petroglyphs in South America show a man with a ray gun in his hand. Another shows a man riding on a machine that has fire coming from its back much like present-day rockets. It is now believed from new evidence that some civilizations had atomic power in the distant past.

The rumors of Atlantis cannot be dismissed as something dreamed up by ancient philosophers in Greece. Why did the Mayans call the Atlantic ocean Atlan before they had ever seen a European? Why do their pyramids so closely resemble the ones in Egypt? Why did the Mayans and Egyptians, who were very primitive people, suddenly within a hundred years become knowledgeable enough to build the most impressive structures ever built by man? These cannot be duplicated today even with your most advanced technology and tools.

Their stone carvings cannot be replicated with your modern equipment. Presumably they had only hardened brass and copper with which to work. You have machines that can lift tremendous weights, yet these people seem to have lifted them with no machines at all. How?

The man in Florida who built the Coral Gardens knew at least part of the secret. He had cut and shaped a column of coral weighing sixty tons and moved it to his garden and stood it on end without the aid of a machine. There was no trailer made capable of carrying sixty tons at this time, so he made one from old car parts, loaded it himself and had a farmer with a tractor pull it to his garden. He unloaded it and stood it on end, and it still stands there today.

During the glacial period, most of the northern continents were covered in ice. This occurred about seventeen thousand years ago. It receded seven to eight thousand years ago. This glacier cap took many thousands of years to form and was a mile thick over the northern continent almost as far down as the equator. Within two thousand years it had all but disappeared. There must have been a very big change in climate to do this.

Can you imagine the weight of this ice being suddenly lifted? The land surely rose afterwards. This must have caused earthquakes never seen before since the beginning of the Earth's formation. The change in climate must have been dramatic. But still man survived this catastrophe. Imagine the dust and carbon monoxide to be contended with. The cultural progress of man was all but destroyed at this time and persisted only in the memory of the survivors.

But this was only a recent ice age. How many have happened before this in times past? How many times has the culture of man been destroyed in this manner?

Many, many, many times, I was told. As long as nature and the Earth revolve there always will be cataclysms. But man himself sometimes causes these terrible things to happen: Covering the land with asphalt and concrete so it can't breathe. Building huge city complexes in one area instead of spreading them out. This causes a huge weight on certain areas that will one day disturb the balance and rotation of the Earth. Some will say that the Earth is so big that it makes no difference. They are wrong. The Earth is delicately balanced on its axis and this weight is tremendous and should cause you concern.

An asteroid hitting the Earth could throw it off balance. Huge bombs going off in certain areas could do the same. Man thinks he is the smartest animal on the Earth, but this is debatable. Everything he creates destroys something else. This will someday soon destroy him. Will there be enough of mankind left to start over again? Perhaps. Perhaps not. After December 23, 2012, according to the Mayan Calender, which so far has proved to be most accurate, history comes to an end.

6. THE OLMEC

Born Many Times was now talking so fast and about so many places that it was difficult for me to understand or grasp some of his statements. He talked of places of which I had no knowledge and times that were beyond my reason. He sensed the confusion in my mind and slowed down, starting to talk of my own time in space. He began:

The Olmec people are the earliest known to you to exist on this continent, but it is known others must have been here before them. Today they are known as the Rubber people, not because they tapped the trees and made rubber, but because they lived where the rubber trees were numerous.

They are better known as the people who made the large basalt stone heads found in their part of the world. But they did not make these stone heads. They were there countless centuries before the Olmec. Even the Olmec did not know the people who made them.

Their legends said that people who were giants made them. Could this be true or believable? Let us say that the conditions on Earth were such that it could produce giant people. What if the atmospheric pressure was below what it is today and, combined with other factors, would allow people to grow larger? What if the specific gravity was less than today? Would this allow people to grow larger? It is not impossible when you think of the large animals that once inhabited the Earth.

It would have taken people with enormous strength to move such large stone heads. The material to make the heads, basalt, was only available some one hundred and fifty miles from where they were found.

But it is apparent that they made the heads round so it would not be impossible for an ordinary-sized man to roll them into position. What is confusing is why they were made in the first place. It appears that they wanted to leave a message for following generations of people so they would know what they looked like.

This only adds to your confusion because they do not look like any of the people presently occupying this area. They have distinctive faces and some look quite oriental. There is no doubt that the Chinese did visit this area many centuries ago. On their heads they seem to be wearing leather helmets similar to what football players wear. None of these races ever occupied this area as far as your historical knowledge is concerned, so who made them?

Perhaps you should give credence to the philosophy that the Earth was visited by people from other planets or realms of consciousness of which you are unaware. This could explain where Quetzalcoatl and Virachoca came from, bringing with them knowledge that was not available anywhere else in the world at that time.

Or should you look at the possibility that there were previous civilizations that were as advanced as your own or even surpassed it? This would probably satisfy most people. But then where did they get their knowledge in such a short time? It was from visitors from Atlantis and Lemuria, whose own landmasses had sunk into the sea.

If a civilization as advanced as your own was suddenly destroyed by a natural cause, such as a large meteor hitting the Earth, an earthquake or a volcano, and only a few survived, could it live again the way it had been used to living?

Suppose something like that happened today and there were only a few hundred survivors left in the world. Could they rely on the water supply? Would there be enough food for them?

The Olmec Sculpture

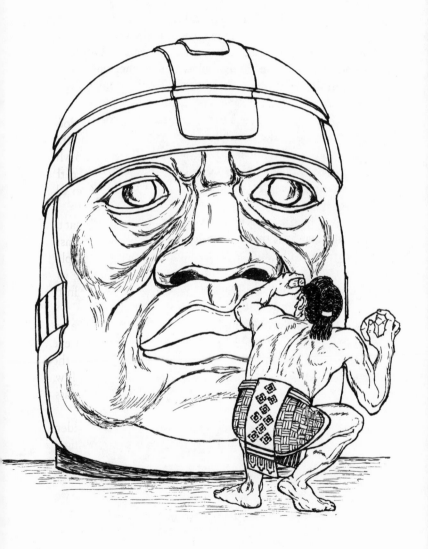

What would they do without electricity or fuel? Machines would be useless. What would they do for clothing and shelter? Would those things that had been important to them before remain important to them now? Frankly, it is probable they would again develop into a primitive society trying to find food and shelter like they had to do many centuries ago.

Education, science, mechanical knowledge, medical experience would not be of any real benefit to you in such a new environment. You would again have to become hunters and gatherers in order to survive. How many times has this happened in the past? Many, many times. Yet the human race has survived and advanced again and again.

This now brings us back to the Olmec. This group of people, with some knowledge which had been given to them from past civilizations, again embarked on the path to civilization. This ended in the Mayan and Aztec cultures that were destroyed by the mindless Spanish conquerors. They were amazed at the cities they saw, greater than those in Europe. Considering them to be pagan, they routinely destroyed them. You will never know the extent of the damage done to present-day knowledge by Cortez and his kind, all in the name of their king and their church.

But do not think this is an isolated incident in history. This has happened time and time again in your history and long before. It will happen again in the future unless mankind learns its lessons and its place in nature and in the universe.

7. TRYING TO SORT IT OUT

By now, my mind was like a soup of many things that Born Many Times had told me. He could see that I was very confused and gave me time to try to digest what he had said. But I could not sort out what I had heard, so he said he would tell me of one particular time in the past that would help me understand. He said this was a time about sixty thousand years ago when he spent a lifetime in a now unknown civilization. His story follows as he told it to me.

My mind is sometimes vague about certain details, but this was a good time when the known world was at peace and mankind was able to progress at an accelerated rate. Great strides had been made to give us greater creature comforts than we had ever experienced.

I was a public administrator in this lifetime, and it was my duty to see that everyone shared equally all the fruits of our labor. This was no small task. Our population numbered well over 300,000 people. We were spread over a large area because each family unit was entitled to about ten acres of land. The size of the home and number of buildings on the acreage were tightly controlled.

When a man and a woman were going to live together they applied for a homesite which was supplied to them at no cost. The size of the house was made to accommodate no more than five persons.

If the couple had more children than the space allowed, it was their problem and they had to make do with what they had.

In this way population was kept to a certain number. There were other benefits to be had if you controlled the size of your family.

Your food and clothing allotments, as well as your accommodation, were keyed to a certain number of people in each unit. The only change allowed was when the parents of the eldest daughter became so old they could not care for themselves. They then moved in with the daughter and her man. Then the oldest of her children took over the unit of the old couple. When one member of the family died for whatever reason, the government replaced him or her with a homeless person of the same age and sex, with the approval of the family unit. This person was usually related.

Each family unit was responsible for growing its own food supply. Corn was the main crop along with squash, potatoes, and tomatoes. All grain had to be assessed by a person from the government, and ten percent of the crop had to be stored in a silo in cases of emergency. This ensured that people had food during a period of drought.

A unit could trade surplus food for other things they required. This was allowed only under special circumstances and was rigorously controlled. It was not legal for anyone to possess more than another person did. This did not stifle ambition because all single-family units were part of a larger unit, and though they were not allowed to gain more from their efforts, they did gain a high rank in the group.

Rank was very important to a family unit. For one thing, their children became more desired by other parents as mates for their children. High rank also meant more respect at the meetings held every month by the government.

A member could become one of the planners, which was the first step toward becoming part of the local government. This was a high honor indeed. Eventually one could, with hard work, become a member of the central government.

Usually a family with older children would help a family with younger ones, and this would make their work easier. A man who helped others was thought of highly. There were not many conflicts among the units. Each knew their responsibility to the other and to the state. Troublemakers were severely dealt with, but this sort of thing rarely occurred.

Many miles away, there were other similar cities and they had contact quite regularly with the residents. There were intermarriages among them and they all lived in harmony. They knew that to the north huge masses of ice covered the Earth and certain people lived near these ice fields to hunt animals they used for food. As the ice receded, the land now exposed quickly grew the food animals lived on. So the meat-eating people had plenty of game.

It was a dangerous place to live because it could become very stormy with winds of great velocity and there were few places to hide. The land was exposed and the trees did not grow big enough to supply shelter. Hurricanes and tornadoes were common. One day it could be very warm and the next very cold. However, people did live there and survive.

In the place where I lived, the temperature was moderate and we were blessed with enough rain for our crops. The land was put to rest after two years of growing so it could replenish itself. Special grasses were grown and dug back into the Earth again to help it to become fertile. We could grow two crops a year from our land.

This gave us time to be active in cultural and religious pursuits. We believed in one god, who was the sun, but he had many servants that we gave homage to. These were the Rain, Earth, and Wind spirits.

Our spiritual leaders had a great influence on us. They kept the many ceremonies believed necessary for our survival. They also had medical knowledge to use when people became sick. Medicines were made from leaves, flowers, and roots of plants. These spiritual leaders were both men and women. Women held an equal position in our society with men.

It was strongly believed that all living things were one and the same, only different in form. Everything somehow benefitted the other in many ways. If some were doing badly, the others would help to make them do well again. So each species helped the other. Most of the people in our area were vegetarians and lived accordingly.

Other people were meat-eaters and they behaved differently. The vegetarians were healthier and had more compassion for each other. The meat-eaters were more aggressive and less hospitable. It was strange how the animals knew the areas where it was safest for them to live. Even the most vicious and man-eating animals treated each of us differently.

8. WATER, WATER EVERYWHERE

As a public administrator, I had to assess the crops grown each year and make sure that some were taken to be stored for the time we might have a crop failure. Fortunately this did not happen for many years. There were some problems with insect invasions, but these were only temporary. Nature would restore the balance before long.

We were aware that the ice shield to our north was retreating at a faster rate than before, because the rivers were swelling above their banks more often. This caused concern because the people near the rivers were in some danger.

Then, suddenly, the water level began to fall once more and the rivers became mere streams again. Since there was the usual amount of rainfall it was a puzzle. We were told that the ice caps up north were not melting as fast so the lack of water that usually came from this was the reason the rivers had subsided.

One morning as I left my home, there was a loud sound or roar to be heard and we began to wonder what it was. Suddenly we could see a huge wall of water coming toward us. It was higher than any hill around. Everyone panicked and many ran for their homes and shut the doors.

I could tell that this was useless because nothing would stop the wall of water. I could see trees and homes being carried toward us as though they had never been on the ground.

I knew it was too late to seek higher ground even if any could be found. To hide would be useless because there was no place to hide. I was beside a small tree and I wrapped my arms around it and held on. The water hit with a terrible rush and I was picked up, tree and all, and sent tumbling and turning around at a very fast speed. I lost my grip on the tree and tried to reach the surface to breathe. I was almost unconscious when I was tossed from the water into the air.

I gasped for breath and landed back in the water. It grabbed me as though with unseen hands and swept me along with terrifying speed. I could see nothing except a glimpse of sky once in awhile. There was no sound except a large roar from the water. A tree swept close to me and I grabbed at its branches.

I managed to get hold of one and pulled myself onto the trunk among the branches. It was well I did, because there was so much debris swirling around me I could have been knocked out and drowned. The tree was continually hitting other objects as it sped along.

I could see other people being swept by, but they were face down or did not move so I felt they were past helping. For two days I clung to the tree and bit by bit the water began to slow its mad rush. The next morning the sun was shining and the warmth was a welcome relief.

After a while I looked around me and was surprised to see another figure above me in the same tree. I called to the person and there was no reply, so I felt by the way the figure was hanging that the person was dead. I looked around me and the water was nearly calm, though there was still a current moving us along.

I reached down for water to drink and found it to be salty. We had been washed out into the ocean, which was miles away from my home. I looked around and saw some coconuts caught in the tree branches. I maneuvered around so I could get one. A branch had broken off near me and, using the stump, I managed to remove the coconut husk and pierce a hole so I could get at the milk.

I drank quickly and then was at a loss as how to get at the meat. I grabbed another nut and removed the husk and drank its milk. With what strength I had I used one nut to crack the other. I felt my strength returning and with the warmth of the sun fell asleep.

I awoke with a start when something brushed past me. I turned to find a girl reaching for some of the coconut meat I had left. I handed it to her and grabbed another from the water. I again removed the husk and pierced a hole in its eye so she could get the milk.

I broke the shell of another nut to get at the meat. She ate slowly, watching me all the while. I asked her if she had suffered any physical injury during our perilous ride and she said she had not. I had suffered a blow to the head, but other than a small cut I was all right.

She climbed higher into the branches, leaving me to wonder where this strange journey was taking us. I collected as many of the coconuts going by as I could reach. There was much debris floating around with the bloated bodies of people and animals drifting by.

Darkness soon fell and I slept fitfully. Morning arrived with the sun shining again. The girl climbed down to where I was perched and we consumed three more nuts. She told me she could see the outline of land to the west but it was not very clear.

I noticed we seemed to be going around in a big circle because the land would change its direction from where we were, sometimes to our north and to our west. This meant we were caught in a huge circular current. During the next few days it became evident that at a certain time we would be closer to the land than before, but soon we would be further away again.

Eventually we came within a half mile of the shoreline and I made plans to try to swim there. The girl could not swim and I was not a strong swimmer. I told her I would get help and come back for her. It was a promise I did not know if I would be able to keep.

The next day when I observed that the land was coming closer I went into the water, swimming with the current for a time. When the current started to swing offshore I had to swim with all my strength to get away from it. I watched the tree slowly disappear from sight.

I was now alone in water still crowded with debris. I had to push things out of my way and proceeded at a slow pace. Darkness overtook me, and the only way I could tell my direction was to listen for the sound of the surf on the shore. I had grabbed a large piece of wood to keep me on the surface during the night. I kept myself awake and tried to move the wood toward the surf.

By morning I was so tired I could not even collect my thoughts. I knew I could not last much longer. I decided to give it one last try and letting the wood go, I swam as fast and strongly as I could.

I could feel my strength leaving me. My breath was more labored and I could not see anything.

Just as I was losing consciousness I felt something grab my hair and drag me through the water. Rough hands dragged me onto the shore just as things turned dark. I have no idea how long I was unconscious, but later I was told by my rescuers that they had given me up for dead. I awoke to find myself lying on the sand without any clothes on whatsoever.

As I came awake, I could smell wood smoke and turned my head to see four men sitting by a driftwood fire. One noticed me and they all came over and helped me to the fireside.

They gave me something to drink that was warm and tasted fishy. They spoke a language that was unfamiliar to me. I began to observe them as they were observing me. They wore small linen aprons and that was all. I learned they had wool blankets they wore over their shoulders when it was cool. Their hair was cut short, barely reaching their ears. Their skin was a pale brown, almost white. They had round faces and stood about five feet high. They smiled a lot, showing strong white teeth, and seemed to be a friendly group.

They gave me some fruit that was familiar to me and a hard biscuit made from some type of plant. After we had eaten they gave me a robe to wear and took me toward the jungle along the shore. There, to my surprise, were stacked dead bodies they had taken from the water. Also in piles were things they could use, such as clothing and furniture.

Apparently they were scavenging from the debris floating in to shore from the storms in my homeland. Many of these items they had never seen before and did not know their use. I soon surmised that they had hoped to get a live survivor like me to show them how to use them. The shoreline was full of more debris so they wasted no more time with me and went back to their scavenging.

I went over to where the dead had been laid out and tried to see if I could recognize any of the people. It was impossible to do. They had become bloated in the water and now in the heat of the sun were decomposing at a rapid rate. Their clothes had been removed, and I could see the victims were in every age group. The stench of this dead flesh became overpowering and I left to go down near the water's edge.

I sat nearby while my rescuers sifted through the debris. They carried the stuff to a pile they had made and returned for more. When they found a dead person they removed the clothes and put any jewelry into a skin bag. Sometimes they found a clay bowl with a plug still secure and full of some grain. This made them shout with satisfaction.

I suddenly realized the robe I was wearing was from one of these unfortunate people. I tore it off and went looking for something more like what my hosts wore. One of the older persons saw me and from a pile of his own clothing gave me an apron such as they used. He showed me how to wear it and I was glad.

I returned to where they had the fire and, finding a straw mat nearby, lay down and was soon asleep. I awoke from my sleep with a start and realized it was morning. Someone had placed a blanket over me to keep me warm. The men had started the fire again and fed me the same food as I had had the day before.

I had not forgotten the promise I had made to the girl in the tree and tried to tell the men about it. They just smiled those damned smiles of tolerance. Finally, by drawing pictures in the sand, I made the one who had given me the apron understand. I drew a picture of a boat and he laughed and showed the other men.

9. A RESCUE MISSION

Soon I began to understand that they had a boat in a stream about a mile away. Later I was to find out it was a dugout canoe. I asked if I could borrow it to rescue my companion and they laughed as usual. But two of the men disappeared and by midday they returned with the canoe. It was about fifteen feet long, made from a red wood.

They made me understand that if the water was calm enough the next morning, two of them would take me out to look for the tree. The next morning at dawn we could see the ocean was calm, so they made ready to go with me. One man filled a gourd with water while another filled a basket with fruit.

They placed me in the center of the dugout making me sit as low in it as I could, while they sat at each end. Balance was very important in this craft and hard for the novice to maintain. They were experienced and had no trouble. They paddled for about three hours before I felt we were far enough from shore. I tried to remember how the shoreline looked the day I started to swim.

They could not believe that I had swum this far. We floated around for an hour before one of them indicated he could see a tree coming our way. I looked in the direction he pointed and could see nothing. He and the other man paddled that way, and within an hour I could barely make out a tree in the water. It took another hour before we got to it.

I could not see the figure of a person on it and thought it was the wrong tree. But one of the men said he thought there was something near the top of one branch, so we paddled alongside. While we held the canoe, he climbed up into the branches and soon returned with a small, pathetic figure.

He laid it by me and I saw it was the girl. They handed me the water and indicated I should try to get her to drink but she would not. They told me to keep trying and we left for the shore. I looked down on the poor face and knew I had to get life into her somehow. I took a mouthful of water and holding her mouth open forced the water from my mouth into it. She coughed and gagged and I knew she might gain consciousness.

She lay quiet for some time and then opened her eyes and looked at me. There was fear in them and I spoke softly to her. She seemed to calm down and in a while took the gourd and drank a small amount of water. Then she went to sleep again. When we made shore just after dark, one of the men there came alongside the canoe and picked her up and carried her to the fireside.

He lay her on the straw mat where I had slept the night before and he took the blanket and covered her. I could tell the way they smiled and looked at me that they were happy for me and the girl. I was to find out later that they thought she was my woman.

The men gave me another mat and a blanket and I lay near the girl in case she needed anything. I could feel the warm sun on my back when I woke up the next morning. I looked over to the girl and she was still asleep. The men had risen early and had gone back to their salvaging.

There was a bowl by the fire with a mixture of grain and oil that these people made their morning meal from. I took some and while I was eating it, the girl woke up and stared at me. I gave her water and asked if she could eat what was there. I gave her the bowl I had and she ate what was left and asked for more. I gave her all there was.

After she had eaten she went to sleep again. I went over to the pile of clothing that the men had salvaged and gathered what I felt she could wear. She had very little on her now so anything would be welcome, I was sure. I placed them on the mat beside her.

I went down to the shoreline and tried to make myself useful. I looked for bowls that had floated in to shore and other things, such as tools. Whenever I came upon a corpse I avoided it. You could tell where they were by the number of birds feeding on them. The birds nearly blocked out the sky, there were so many.

When I returned to the camp I was surprised to see about fifty more people there than when I had left. They appeared to be the same kind of people as the ones who had befriended me and had helped me save the girl. There were men, women, and children in the group. They wore the same clothes as the men I was with.

They were smiling, talking, and laughing together when I appeared. They made me feel welcome and I could see that some of the women were attending the girl, who was happy to find her own gender.

When she saw me she beckoned for me to come over to her. She grabbed my arm and pulled me down beside her. She held my hand as she tried to communicate with the women around us.

I could see she had used some of the clothes I had placed beside her. I told the girl it was sometimes easier to draw pictures in the sand and this she did. Soon all the women were drawing pictures in the sand. So in this way they communicated.

When it became dark a larger fire was made and a meal prepared.

The food was different from what we had eaten in our homeland. They ate meat, which we did not, and some women gave us vegetables and fruit. They had grains that we had never tasted before and root vegetables that had a sweet taste. We enjoyed them.

They started to sing and dance to drums, and it was very entertaining to the girl and me. She was asked to get up and participate and she did, and later told me how much she enjoyed it. As quickly as the festivities had started, they ended, and everyone went to sleep. Some just squatted by the fire while others lay on straw mats. The girl and I had to share the same mat since they thought we were man and woman.

10. THE RESCUERS' VILLAGE

The next morning, the whole camp began to carry some of the salvaged material to the river where they had many canoes lining the shore. The girl and I carried our share and when the boats were loaded they put us into one of the canoes and paddled upstream. They left several people behind to continue the salvaging.

The girl and I paddled along with the other four people in the canoe. It had been made from a single tree and was about twenty-five feet long. There were fifteen canoes in our group. The water was calm and the trip uneventful. As we glided through the jungle, which was thick and dark and filled with the sound of birds and other animals, I saw monkeys swinging among the trees.

The second day we were met by other people in canoes coming to greet us. I could smell wood smoke long before we came to the village. What a village it was! Not a place of poles and grass roofs, but buildings made of square stone blocks. Some were one storey high, but many had two storeys. They were many shapes and sizes. But it was the different colors they were painted that amazed us. There were pinks, blues, greens, yellows, and every color imaginable. The roofs were flat and the walls straight. Some were square, others rectangular, and others had rooms attached to their sides. They seemed to be in every size and shape. They had open doorways and windows. Trees had been planted and gardens flourished everywhere.

A Coastal Fisherman

There was stone pavement between the buildings and there was water running in stone-lined canals everywhere. Every area had a small stone pool of water where the people could get their water supply for their homes. The stone blocks had been covered with a coating of mud or plaster that had been painted. The roofs were flat and below the outside walls. Here and there the ends of the timbers that supported the roof beams protruded.

Both men and women wore the apron-like cover and were bare otherwise. Some of the older women wore a short tunic over their chests. Everyone had a blanket with a hole in the middle that they wore when it was cool. The weather here was usually very warm, but the evenings became cool. All of them wore their hair short-cropped and looking like a bowl on their heads. During the afternoons each person had a favorite spot to just sit in the shade and relax.

The girl, whom I later learned was named Andira, and I were given lodging in a small house with an older couple who were very friendly. We soon learned that we were not just guests of this couple but were their servants and had to care for them. I guessed the man was in his sixties and the woman in her late fifties. They treated us well and were no trouble for us, considering our plight.

It soon became obvious that I was more educated than others around me, and I was taken to another larger village. This new place was inhabited by many thousands of people and the townsite covered many acres of land. The buildings were larger and much more pretentious. This was a government center, and I was later to learn it was the center of science and higher learning.

11. A NEW LIFE

I could now understand some of their language and was better prepared when I was taken to one of the larger buildings and interviewed by three older men. The room was large and contained only one table and several chairs. I was told to sit on one side, and when the three men entered they sat facing me. They wore identical white robes which covered them to the floor. I would guess their ages were between forty and fifty years.

They sat and studied me as I studied them. They smiled and asked if I would like something to drink. I said I would, and a warm drink that I had never had before was served to us by a woman servant. It was sweetened with honey and tasted musty. I learned later it was called chocolate and was made from a bean that grew in the forest nearby. We all sat silently while we drank.

Two women servants appeared, and one removed the cups we had drunk from and the other gave each of us a damp cloth with which to wipe our hands and mouth.

One of the men said something to one of the women, and soon another man came into the room with rolls of cotton in his arms. He spread one on the table, and they indicated that I should look at it. I stood and examined the cloth, which was about four feet square and made of the white cotton. There were lines on it made by something black.

I was puzzled by what I was to make of it and one of the men laughed. He told me it was a map, which still meant nothing to me.

He then explained to me that this was a drawing of the Earth where we lived. He showed me the landmass and the water that surrounded it. He pointed out the rivers and streams that flowed through it and the mountains and trees that grew there. He pointed out where we were located, and I was amazed. I asked him how such a thing could have been made. He told me it was a copy of one found many thousands of years before by his people that had been drawn on a sheet made from the fiber from a grain.

He further stated that they had many more of these maps showing other landmasses that were unknown to them. He could see that I was having difficulty absorbing all he had said, and he told me they would leave me with the keeper of the maps so I could become familiar with them and could learn their purpose. They quietly withdrew, and I began a search that was impossible to comprehend the meaning of. Carefully, the map keeper explained everything he knew about the map before me.

He showed me where I had been rescued from the ocean, and we traced back to where I had probably lived. I told him of the ice glaciers that covered the land to our north, and he took out some white powder and showed me where the ice cap had been. I asked him how he knew this, and he said they had been told by their ancestors from a time long ago.

He said they had written records of this, along with the maps. I was close to being overwhelmed by all that I was learning, and he left for a moment and returned to tell me I could go to my quarters and rest.

One of the woman servants entered the room and took me to a room that was assigned to me during my stay here. I was told to rest and that I would be given a meal before I retired that night.

I was awakened by a servant at dusk and given a meal of fresh fruits and vegetables. I wondered how they knew I was a vegetarian and thought that they had been told by my rescuers. They also gave me a drink made of several different fruits that was delicious. I studied the map that had been left with me and now was able to read it a little better. I was again surprised at the size of the landmass that we lived on. I had known before that there were large bodies of salt water on each side of the land I had lived on, but did not know they were so far apart.

The next morning at daybreak, I was shown where I could bathe and dress. I was given a robe that was all one piece. It was made of a white cotton and was like the blankets the women wore. It had a hole in the center where you put your head through, and it hung down in front and back. There were ties along each side where it was secured together. It hung to just below my knees. I was given almost the same meal as I had the night before. The only difference was the grain had been soaked in some kind of light oil.

I returned to the room where the three men and the map keeper waited for me. They showed me where my village had been before it was drowned. One of the men explained what had happened. The ice cap had been melting, and the ice underneath the cap had melted first, leaving a huge cavern under the cap.

This cavern had caved in and formed a huge dam that held back the water beneath the cap. Eventually, there had been an enormous amount of water held back. The dam had finally given way, and the water had gone on a rampage following the valleys toward the ocean, taking everything in its path. Unfortunately, our village had been a victim of this flooding. They showed me on the map how this had come about and where I had come ashore. I asked how they knew this and they replied that they had scientists that knew these things.

12. MY WORLD GROWS

Again I was left with the map keeper, who had more maps that gave a closer look at the area where I had lived. He explained that the ice cap had influenced the weather patterns where we both lived and, with the ice cap melting, they were becoming concerned about sudden Earth changes they knew would happen. There were two main matters of concern. One was the tremendous amount of water being put into the ocean by the melting ice. They estimated that the ocean's shorelines already had risen approximately twenty-six feet and they knew it would get much higher than that. Many of their villages by the ocean had already been flooded.

The second and larger concern was that the weight of three miles of ice being removed from the surface of the Earth would make profound changes to the landmass. They expected Earth movements and volcanoes erupting, creating earthquakes on a mammoth scale. Life as they knew it was at great risk. There would be climatic changes that could destroy vegetation in places where it would take centuries to stabilize again. This would cause food shortages for forms of life depending on this vegetation for survival.

I was aghast at what he was saying and completely demoralized. I knew what I had just been through myself and realized what he said was true. I thought of my family and others I had known and knew within me that the girl, Andira, and I were the only ones that had survived.

There may have been others but these people knew of none. I asked to be allowed to go outdoors to digest what I had learned and he agreed.

I was shown down a passageway to a courtyard where flowers and trees grew in profusion. I chose a bench by a wall in the sunlight and sat there in the warmth of the sun. In a far corner children were laughing and playing. It was hard to believe that such tragedies would be the fate of the world in the near future. I looked at the flowers growing close by and the trees that were blooming and wondered if they would survive.

I must have dozed off because I became aware with a start that a servant was touching my arm. She had a dish with fruit and a sweet roll made of the grain that was used here extensively. I knew it was sweetened with honey and had been baked by a fire because it was still warm. There was juice to drink as before.

One of the men whom I had first met when I arrived at this center approached and sat beside me on the bench. He asked if I was being treated well, and I told him everything was more than satisfactory. He then asked what I would like to do now that I was among them. I did not hesitate for a moment and said that I would like to stay with them in this building and study the maps and any other documents they had to do with the past civilizations of man.

He explained that it would not be easy to get permission for this and I would have to have a good reason for my request. I told him that this was where my interests lay and I thought I could come up with some valuable information for them as well as satisfy my own curiosity.

He promised to see what he could do to get the necessary permission. In the meantime, he said, they would have no objections if I looked at the maps they had in their library in this building. He told me it was a very small amount of the material they had at the central scientific complex nearby.

I took advantage of his suggestion and spent the next week scanning all the documents they had in the library. The more I found, the more I wanted to find. I was looking at a different world with all this information available. It showed many other landmasses that we had not known existed. It showed these landmasses joined together in one large mass then, on another map, separated into individual landmasses with huge bodies of water in between them.

It showed large areas completely covered in vegetation and then the same area completely devoid of any vegetation. There were places where the land was joined to another by a land bridge and the same area on another map showed an island without any joining land bridge. There were flat plains of land and then on another map, the same area had become a moun- tainous region. As I studied these maps with the map keeper I became aware that this was to be a long complex study.

I could hardly wait to get to the main library and begin my pursuit of knowledge. I was given permission to go there within a few days. I was taken to the largest building in the city. I now realized how huge this place was. It had been very deceiving when I arrived here. The city covered a large valley between two high mountain ridges. The climate was temperate the year round. Surrounding the city were farms producing a large variety of foodstuffs.

Fruit trees covered the lower slopes of the mountains on each side. I could see some animals in a field some distance away but could not tell what type they were.

I was given a room in an extension from the main area where the work was done. An eating area was nearby. Every morning it was compulsory to bathe first, then go to a certain area to sit quietly and meditate for a while before having a meal. The day started at sunrise and ended at sunset.

The library was immense. Documents were written on paper made from vegetation and leather, and clay tablets and stone, which were engraved with petroglyphs. There were many strange languages used. I was told some of the documents went back thousands of years. My main interest was the maps, and there were a lot to see. They covered a whole section of the library.

There were two other people in the section with me—an older man and a young boy. I was given a table to work at near an opening in the outer wall. This gave me light and a good view of the hills nearby. During the next days, I worked tirelessly going over old maps and documents. I asked the older man to help me with the languages that I could not understand, and sometimes we had to ask another person who was an expert. Some of these documents were very old indeed.

They showed the part of the world where I had lived as it had been many centuries before. There had not been a solid landmass from east to west like it now was, but two long islands separated by another sea.

On further discussions with another expert, I was told that the top of the Earth now was actually near the bottom, and the part now covered in an ice cap was once tropical.

13. ANOTHER WORLD ENDS

I was so entranced with the information that was available to me that I did not notice changes going on around me until informed by the others. This came about one morning when we had some ground tremors that shook the building where I was working. They did no real damage, but they scared me.

I was told that these had been becoming more numerous during the past year and they were concerned. Sometimes grey dust settled on everything and the river nearby became cloudy with mud. They told me there must be volcanoes erupting in the interior of the country. So far the tremors had done little damage, but they were cause for grave concern.

I continued my work, because it was useless to fear the unknown. After what I had been through earlier, I felt that if anything did happen I would just have to cope with it the best way I could. Many people who had lived through earthquakes and volcanoes in the past left for other areas they felt would be safer, but I wanted to stay where the things I studied were available.

Little did I or others know the terrible catastrophe that was coming. Trembling of the land became more frequent and more dust would fill the air until sometimes we had difficulty breathing. We would cover our faces with cloth masks to make breathing easier. People coming into our city told us it was the same no matter where they tried to hide from it.

Then one evening it happened. There was a terrible earthquake and many buildings collapsed. My building was badly damaged and I suffered cuts and bruises. I went out into the street and helped to dig people out from collapsed buildings. I think it must have been close to sunrise when the sky brightened up with what seemed to be a fire.

It lasted only a moment then another terrible quake hit with such fury it threw me through the air. I landed among large stones and knew I had broken bones. People were screaming all around me. I could hear cries for help but they were soon smothered by what seemed to be a wall of Earth falling upon us. I knew that it was dust from a volcano so thick it seemed a solid mass. I was choking for air and soon lost consciousness and died.

So ended a lifetime where there was much human development and progress that was not really lost because strange as it might seem, there were survivors to tell about this time. Only because of the ignorance of future generations did these records become lost to mankind for a long time to come.

14. MORE INFORMATION

It was some time before Born Many Times again contacted me. I think he wanted to give me time to think about what he had told me so far. This time he wanted to take me to another place in history about three thousand years before the present. He said that it would make me understand more fully what the progress of man was like in the past and why. He informed me this would be unbelievable to most people today because we think and act differently from the way people in the past did. In his opinion we are more skeptical and have a religious mind-set that is difficult to penetrate.

He asked me how I thought mankind managed to survive for so many millions of years before it had the many different religious beliefs that it has today. He told me that mankind always had a belief in something, be it animals, serpents, plants, trees, planets, stars, or spirits of the dead and other mystical things. The most important of these was the sun. Mankind realized that the sun made things grow and supplied the moisture to give them life. Without the sun they knew there could be no life.

This led us to the next subject, the lifetime of the Inca. These people lived on the west coast of South America. Usually, they occupied the flat coastal regions, but many lived in the valleys and inland plains. Others lived among the mountain ranges and on the slopes of the mountains where they had terraced gardens. They were, up to the time of "The Coming", mostly farmers and because of this they worshiped the sun.

"The Coming" was the landing of strange beings who were not of this world. Today they would be called aliens from another planet. I know this will shock most of the readers, but that was the way it was. The people who came looked the same as you do even today. There was nothing strange or threatening about them, except their clothing and means of transportation.

The transportation was large metal tubes that defied gravity. They needed space to land just as modern aircraft do today. Their clothes were made of a fine cloth of brilliant colors. Naturally, the natives thought these people were god's representatives from the sun. Despite the denial of this from the visitors, the primitive minds of the natives would accept no other explanation.

The visitors wanted to trade for certain metals that were plentiful in the area and in return for this they would show the natives many things to help them grow more and better food, build with stone and refine metal for tools. Many metals were readily available to the natives, such as copper, iron, silver, and gold. They would be taught how to separate the metal from stone and gravel, refine it and, in some cases, blend it for strength.

In farming the visitors had with them seeds of many different plants to grow for their benefit. The natives already grew tubers of potatoes, squash, pumpkin, tomatoes and maize. They showed them how to treat the soil so it would not become unproductive, how to rotate their planting and to cross-breed plants for other varieties of food.

They showed them how to combine different grains both domestic and wild, to produce more plentiful crops, and to give variety.

During the stays of these visitors, who were coming and going for more than the next hundred years, the natives learned more than they had for the past thousand years or so. They now had food in abundance and tools that made farming easier. They lived in buildings which were well-constructed. Their population was expanding because they were healthier and food was getting more plentiful.

But eventually the visitors left them. The people were surprised because many had mated with them and so they thought that they never would leave. It was a time of great depression for them, but a few of the better-informed soon took over and they kept the knowledge of what they had learned.

They still believed that these visitors had come from the sun and they worshiped the sun even more now. They reasoned that they should build temples to the sun. Like the Egyptians and Maya, they felt that they ought to become as close as possible to the sun. So instead of pyramids, they built their temples on the mountaintops where they are still found today. It was not possible for them to grow enough food in these religious villages so high up so food was brought to them from the gardens below.

The visitors had taught them to build roads, and these are still evident today. They run almost the length of the western coast from the north to the south. They were used as trade routes and the llama was used as the beast of burden.

They had the wheel available to them, but they found that ten llamas could carry more than any wagon they could build. Besides, a llama gave you food and wool. A wagon gave you broken wheels on the stone pavement.

They had built certain roads for the visitors to land on and they now made many more to try to entice them to return. They even built large pictographs which are only discernable from a great height to show the visitors the way to the landing roads. Many other groups of people left messages in large pictographs that can only be seen from the air.

To deny that these drawings were meant to be seen by viewers from a great height is foolish and unrealistic. How else were they to be viewed? They are not discernable from the land they are on. To have made the drawings is an engineering feat worthy of respect. To make straight lines for such great distances and over obstacles is a tremendous accomplishment, especially without the engineering tools available today.

How and where did they acquire these skills? Did they really slowly evolve over time? Did they learn to cut and shape huge stones with such accuracy by trial and error? Did they learn metallurgy the same way? Did they learn to make items of silver and gold of such beauty and intricate design in a short time? The answer is that they were shown these skills by someone who had this knowledge to begin with. How else could all this be accomplished in such a short time by a primitive, farming people?

Perhaps mankind should begin to realize that we are not alone in the universe. This means the outer universe that is around us in countless planets and stars. It also means the inner universe that we all have within us.

They both exist and are with us, helping mankind to reach his true destiny. Admitting they exist and are a part of our being is a good start on this road.

15. ARE WE ONLY TEMPORARY?

By now my mind was a mush of information. Should I believe that this person was telling me truths or just being philosophical? If he had lived all the lives he claimed and remembered, why doesn't everyone remember? I asked him this question and he laughed at me.

"Do you not remember your other lives?" he asked me.

I told him I had trouble remembering what I did last week, never mind other lives.

Again he laughed and began a long conversation about before- and after-lives which I will repeat as much as I can remember.

Born Many Times continued:

It is inconceivable to me that man cannot understand that he is but a small part of a Greater Being. This Being is in each person when he or she is born. It is the one part of you that can never be destroyed. You are part of a Greater Intelligence that you are capable of contacting and using anytime. The only thing you must do is realize that you are part of this Being and Intelligence.

In this way you can make greater use of who you are. But, then too, you must also realize that all living things are part of this Being and Intelligence. You must respect all living things, for each has a purpose and need for your survival.

There are only two types of living things. Those that live as flesh and those that live as vegetation.

Those of the flesh are mobile and able to move from place to place. Those of vegetation are stationary and cannot move around except in a very limited way like vines or through seeds borne on the wind from place to place. These must get nourishment from the soil.

At first mankind ate only vegetation, but as time went on he began to eat the flesh of other animals. Many living animals eat the flesh of others. But there are some that eat nothing but vegetation. Mankind has no need to eat the flesh of others, and many people do not.

During the history of humankind many things have been worshiped, but the most common were different species of animals. A few peoples worshiped different types of vegetation, but these were rare occurrences. Most worshiped the sun as the giver of all life. And it is the giver of life because without it all life as we know it would cease.

Man always had to believe in some type of superpower to survive the thought of death. Now man worships himself in the form of a holy person or one who is godlike in his image. Humans have always worshiped those things or beings that are most important to them. Now, in this time, it is himself he worships in the form of a man.

Mankind forgets that without the sun and Earth and all natural things, he could not exist, saying instead that these are just things god created for him to use to survive.

Perhaps he should realize that he was created so that nature as well would survive, and that was why he was given more intelligence than any other living thing so he could accomplish this for the good of all living things as well as his own good.

Humans must realize that to survive they have to become conscious of the needs of other living creatures whose being here is for their benefit as well. This brings us to the way some peoples handled their relationship with nature, which was far different from the way it is done in your time. It is well known by all of us that the people living in the "New World", as it was known to early explorers, lived with nature in a way that was destroyed by these explorers. These "heathen" and "uncivilized" people were to be converted to the "true" religion of these explorers.

Let us not forget that these "heathens" worshiped the Great Spirit who was the same as your god. But they worshiped a Spirit that was manifested in all living things and did not attach to themselves a human element to be worshiped. They believed that all living things had a Spirit that was related to and part of the Great Spirit. And with this thought, that all living things were related to them also.

Whenever they took the life of another living thing they asked forgiveness and explained that now its Spirit would be part of the Spirit to live on in them. Is it so hard to understand this? When all living things exist because of the sun energy given them, they pass this energy on when they are eaten by another.

When a person died, he or she became a Spirit, so during their burial, food and tools were buried with them. The food was to sustain them on their voyage.

Naturally they could not eat the food, but when the food was dead they could then eat the food's Spirit. When a person was sick, the shaman, by making a noise with rattles, making a sacred smoke, and beating drums, attracted the Spirits necessary to heal the sick person. He knew that the Spirits of other living things have the power to heal. Because they are all part of the same Spirit, they can heal each other.

16. GREY FOX

Born Many Times knew that I was completely confused by his statements, so he told me he would let another man, Grey Fox, tell the story of life as an Indian and describe what he went through. Grey Fox's story is the same as those Born Many Times had listened to for hundreds of years when he lived among the native peoples. Grey Fox began:

My name is Grey Fox and I was born to Wounded Elk and Happy Laughter who were part of the Iroquois tribes. I was born in the early spring in a longhouse with many people present. This is an account of what it meant to be a First Nations person. I cannot remember everything that happened to me, so I must go by what happened to each of us when we were born into this period of time and this tribe.

My mother, with the help of other women, cleaned me with soft dried moss and warm water. They did this by holding the water in their mouths until it was warm then spitting it on me. Mother held me all this time and put me to her breast as soon as was possible. In this way I bonded with her. Her constant care the first few months of my life made me aware that this was the person who cared most for me and kept me warm and fed.

This first bonding was to remain important to me all my life. The next bonding I experienced was with the other women in the longhouse who also had small children like me. When I was able to move, first by crawling or by dragging my little bottom across the earthen floor, I was continually picked up and held by other women. They would let me take their breast while they held me.

My next bonding was with other small children who were close to my age or a little older. I grew up with these children and they influenced my life. My other adult influence was my father, but he was away so much in my younger years that I only saw him occasionally, and so we did not become close as my mother and I did. When she went out to work in our garden she would prop me against a tree and work for hours, carrying water and pulling weeds.

When I was a little older I played with other children my age. While our mothers worked in the garden we would explore the fields or forest nearby under the watchful eye of an older woman or a young girl. Sometimes an older man would watch us and show us many wondrous things that we could make. All of them told us stories which kept us fascinated for hours. Many older children, still too young to work in the garden for long periods of time, would come and show us new games to play.

During long, cold winter days in the longhouse we played games and were entertained by older men or women. As I grew I was given small chores to do and, like all children, enjoyed these little jobs because they kept me occupied and I knew they contributed to the good of all the clan. We were never disciplined with anger or violence by our elders, but were shamed by not being included in the tribal goings-on until we straightened up. If one wanted to be included in the community, one had to do one's share.

We learned these things early because it was important to belong somewhere. To be excluded by the other children your age from games was a terrible punishment which not many children wanted to incur. Many of the older people would counsel us on proper behavior, and as children, we respected their knowledge. Our longhouse contained our closest relatives, and there was much love and respect among us for each other. No one wanted to lose that love and respect. In the other longhouses it was the same, even though some were larger and some smaller.

When I grew a little older, I began to bond with people from the other longhouses because they were part of our larger community. I was soon to learn that what affected one of us affected everyone. We in the village were all one when anything came up that mattered, which was usually always. I made good friends in each of the longhouses and we visited back and forth. Within your own longhouse you were welcomed at every fire pit and given whatever there was to eat. Of course we soon learned who had the best food and who was the best cook.

When I was young there was no difference made whether we were male or female. Later, the only difference was the type of work we were told to do. The head of the longhouse was the Clan Mother and her word was final. Not even the men dared to ignore what she had to say.

Our Clan Mother was very old, but very sweet. Her smile was contagious and everyone loved her. Many times she would sneak up on me and give me such a hug it would take my breath away. She said every child in our longhouse was hers. There was not a child that could help but love her as much as they did their real mother, or for that matter, all the women of the tribe. In our tribe the word for mother was the same for aunts and all the other women of our clan.

The first animals I bonded with were the dogs. They were everywhere in the longhouse. Who they belonged to or where they came from, no one seemed to care. They belonged to everybody in the longhouse where they were staying at the time. Some dogs would be in our longhouse for a while then suddenly disappear and show up in another longhouse in the village. A dog had puppies near our sleeping bunks one spring and they fascinated me. I would play with them for hours. My mother said my face had never been so clean as it was from the constant licking it got from the pups.

These pups grew fast and soon they were outside with their mother. Naturally all the dogs had fleas and these were a problem for us, too. Our only relief from them came in the cold months of winter. Our bedding was made up of furs and they had their own colonies of fleas that plagued us. When the warm weather came in the spring the fleas got competition from the mosquitoes and black flies. Not everything was idyllic about our lives, but we learned to live with small discomforts.

I found out how to swim early in my life. Being in the water helped avoid the pests. Playing in the water was one of the most pleasant things we did. But there were many other things to occupy us every day. We needed to learn to make the things necessary for living, like tools and weapons.

When I was not playing or learning to make things, I was always going to fetch something. It seemed like I was constantly going for water, going for firewood, going to pick berries or nuts, going to get beans or squash or something else from the garden, going to look for my sisters or brothers.

After the evening meal in the longhouse in winter, or outside when the weather permitted, we had story-telling time. This was when we learned about the tribe's history and the accomplishments of some of our people. We had many story-tellers in our tribe, and sometimes a visitor from another tribe would bring new stories for us to hear. Sometimes a woman would be a story-teller and she usually told about the good deeds of women, while the men told stories about men. I heard the same stories over and over and would usually fall asleep before the familiar ones were finished.

There were many ceremonies held by the fire pits at night, and some of these I was not allowed to attend until I got older.

There were also secret meetings and ceremonies held in special places by different groups of the men. These men never divulged anything about the ceremonies, and anyone who did was never seen again. Every longhouse was named for the clan that lived there. Some of the names were The Wolf, The Bear, The Dog and other animal names.

Our longhouse was called The Bird for our clan. Our ceremonies featured the dress and actions of birds. Many colored feathers and bird claws were used. Capes, dresses, and head covers were made of the skins and feathers of birds.

The Story-Teller

Birds were considered sacred to us and we had several types of them in cages that we used in ceremonies.

By the time I was old enough to be given my secret name and brought into manhood I had been taught that I was part of many things. I was one with the people of my tribe and all of mankind.

I was also one with all other life forms existing in my world. I knew that all life was important, from the trees to the fish in the water, and that they all belonged to the Great Spirit even as I did. I was part of them, and they were part of me.

In preparation for the manhood ceremony, I had to attend learning classes along with many other young boys. The shaman who taught us was respected by our tribe for his knowledge and goodness.

I shall explain part of the lessons as he gave them to us. The Builder of all things that exist—the universe, the stars and all life that inhabits them—we know as the Great Spirit who wanted life to be balanced. When He created one type of life form, He made others that would keep its number in balance with the other life forms. He did this by giving these life forms just so much time to live, but He also gave them the ability to create more of their kind.

He did this because of the need for their species to survive. He gave the rabbits the ability to create more of their kind than other animals did, because they were the prey of so many other life forms. Thus, the ability of other life forms to create depended on the availability of their food sources. If there were not many rabbits, there would not be many foxes or other animals that used them as the backbone of their diet. Therefore, there was always a balance.

Many animals eat only the flesh of others to survive, while others eat only vegetation. Man is an animal that can eat both as is necessary. At one time our ancestors ate only vegetation, and they were more healthy and less aggressive. When they changed their diet to eat meat as well, they became more open to disease and more aggressive.

The people who lived far to our north were more meat-eaters than we were. Their climate did not allow a long growing season, so their vegetation was limited. We knew these people were constantly involved in warfare. Our closer northern neighbors had a better growing season, much as we did. They could grow part of their food in gardens. We, too, still needed meat because we could not raise enough vegetation to keep us fed all the time.

So we turned to the animals in our neighborhood to provide us with meat. These animals ate the vegetation, so we in turn were eating the vegetation that they had consumed. The deer, elk, caribou, buffalo, and moose were the largest and biggest suppliers of our meat. But there were also smaller animals like beaver, porcupine, rabbit and many others that supplemented our diet.

These animals also provided us with fur to keep us clothed and provide shelters and warmth from the weather. Their bones supplied material for tools. We also took the fish from the waters around us. They provided us with a large part of our food supply. We always remembered that the Great Spirit provided us with these sources of food, and we knew we needed to thank and respect each living thing.

We believed that all living things are equal in the eyes of the Great Spirit. As humans, we might have thought we were closer to the Great Spirit than other life, but that was wrong. He made each of us with a specific purpose and we needed to obey His laws.

Not to respect the life of all things means there will eventually be no life. That is why you are here today to hear my words and to learn for your own survival.

Living together, our people learned that we must share, because that was the only way we could survive. We learned to share within our own clans and then within our own tribe. We also learned to share with other tribes that we came into contact with. This had become our way of life. We learned to realize we must also share our world with the other creatures who live here. Not to do so would mean none of us would survive.

This was not just a wish on our part, but the way we knew we must be. It was the way the Great Spirit who had made us had ordered. Not to do as he says was not acceptable. If we took the life of any creature, including man, we had to ask the Great Spirit to forgive us. We needed to also ask the forgiveness of that from which we had taken away life. If they refused to forgive us, or if we failed to ask forgiveness, we would live a very unhappy existence. It is true we took the life of animals, but we did it only for food and clothing. Even then we knew we had to ask forgiveness from that animal or fish and explain to it that it still lived within us and would be treated with great respect.

This is the way that all of the young men were taught to bond with the Great Spirit and our way of living.

After a few days of these lessons from the shaman, we were brought into manhood and given the privileges that went with it. It was now up to each of us to live what we had learned. Because we were expected to obey the rules and respect the laws did not mean that we were to give up our individuality. Each of us were to do what we wanted to do.

Most of us had our heros who were great hunters or warriors and sports figures. Some of the most respected people in the tribe were those who showed excellence in making certain things that we needed.

For instance, a woman who made a certain kind of pottery that was above average was well thought of. Though many people might make exactly the same kind of bowl with the same decoration on it, hers could be instantly recognized. The same went for tools. A man could make projectile points, and though many made the same kind of points, his would be recognized because they were always the best, even though they might look pretty much the same.

We recognized that anything made by a person had that person's energy within the object and could be easily recognized. All native people could recognize this energy and know who the person was who had made the object. We lived so close to one another that we could recognize people by their energy.

When we were in the forest and came upon a campsite that had recently been abandoned, we could tell who had used it by the energy still there. To us, there was no mystery to this.

If we saw bent grass we could tell what animal had passed that way and when. After all, nature was our home and we lived close to her. Our powers of observation augmented our senses of sight and smell, which were as acute as those possessed by any other living animal.

Though our life span was short— thirty to forty years— we made the most of every minute. Much of our time had to be spent gathering food, hunting, fishing, and making shelters to live in. We found a mate early and had children whom we loved and cared for. Our elders were also loved and cared for when they could no longer take care of themselves.

Most of our ceremonies were performed to thank the Great Spirit for something, or to ask His help. At certain times we also had ceremonies for the dead. At the beginning of the growing periods and after the harvesting, a thankful ceremony was held. There was very little that we did not take the time to thank the Great Spirit for.

Many of the men belonged to secret societies that gave them a fellowship and a hope for better-than-average success in what they did. There was one group called the Moon Walkers that had a bad reputation among the people. These men would meet at a secret location at night when the moon was full. It was said that they sacrificed live animals and sometimes even captives at their ceremonies.

No one knew for sure who the members were because they would not admit to anything about it. We could only surmise who belonged when they would be absent from home at this time of the moon. They were a cult feared by many, and if someone knew a member he would avoid him.

There were other secret groups, but not any we felt were as sinister as these were. Many did good things for the people. Others just kept to themselves, having special places where it was believed there was a source of power. Some used stone circles that meant something to them. This does not mean all stone circles were used like this. Some tribes held ceremonies in such circles.

The native people of our tribe had no written language, only a spoken language. So in order to record certain events, they had to use what was close at hand. In some tribes they had a wampum belt. By placing beads in a certain pattern, the tribe related its history. It took a special wampum reader to understand the story in this belt. A tribe near ours had birch bark writing, which was unusual.

In other tribes, stones placed in a circle were used to record the tribe's history. They had a central stone that represented the center of their world as they knew it. Around this in a larger circle were placed stones representing all the members of the tribe. Each tribal member had a stone.

When the tribe got bigger the stone circle also got bigger. Once a year, when all the tribe was assembled at a special ceremony, stones were added to the circle or taken out, whichever was necessary. The stones removed were for the people who had died, and a special place was made for their stones to go. New stones were put down for new babies. The stones for the most important people of the tribe were in the inner circle and the others were in the outer circle. Some special stones were placed according to the sunrise and sunset, for the growing periods and for other things of special importance.

Stone piles in the plains were made for different reasons. Some were piles marking a certain trail. Others were put there for other reasons. The plains Indians needed the buffalo in order to live. When no buffalo were available, the men had to hunt for anything else that could be eaten.

That meant they might even hunt for the tribe's friend, the rattlesnake or any other snake. Sometimes small rodents were eaten. By piling stones together, homes were made for these creatures, and whenever one had to have a snake or rodent to eat he would go shopping in the closest stonepile.

Some people would not eat a rattlesnake, not because they thought it distasteful, but because they believed the snake was sacred. But sometimes they would take a rattler to a gopher hole and have the snake chase the gopher out so they could catch it. The gopher would be eaten and the rattler would be returned to the stone pile unharmed.

As is true everywhere, not all native people were good, and these, though few, were severely dealt with. The most terrible punishment was to be banished from the tribe and its territory forever. No native person was equipped to live without a community around him and with such punishment he or she could seldom survive long."

Born Many Times now resumed his explanation:

I have tried to let you know what a native Iroquois was like and how we lived. There is no mystery about the things we did. We had no special powers, although some shamans appeared to have mysterious abilities. We cultivated our senses and used them to survive. What we did have was a kinship with Mother nature and the Great Spirit. We did not try to control nature, but were content to be controlled by and live in harmony with her. All our ceremonies held to this.

The shaman was a very important person in our society and he did have the ability to bring together the forces of Mother nature to do many wondrous things. In this work he had the help of the medicine woman who knew all the herbs and plants and could make powerful medicines to cure the sick.

During all lives all people walk different paths, but we all end up the at same place.

17. CREATION

I now realized that the information given me by Born Many Times could be better understood if one were to let one's preconceived notions about life and religion in general be kept from one's mind. He now suggested that I could learn something more about the true beginning of man if I opened my mind to what he was about to tell me. He continued:

When the Great Spirit sat down to rest from creating the Universe, He wondered what He should do next. He had a great void full of stars, planets and leftover debris. He then realized that was all He did have, a void with no life. So He decided that He would create life to live somewhere in this void.

Then He wondered what would He make this life out of. It had to be able to move, swim or walk, and grow. He had a lot of surplus energy, so it seemed all He had to do was make a container to hold the energy and the container would then have life. Then he had to create something that would make more energy, and the sun was made.

Now came the problem of how to get this energy from the sun into the container. First He had to make the Earth just at the right distance from the sun so it would not burn up. Then, He had to make something to shade the Earth from some of the harmful rays the sun gave off, so he created an atmosphere for the Earth. This atmosphere would also serve to supply a new element He called oxygen, which would help life and more elements or combinations He called nitrogen, hydrogen, carbon dioxide and many more, all necessary for life, because these elements were used to make the container for life.

Some of these containers of energy He made into vegetation such as grass, trees, and other life forms that took the energy directly from the soil the Earth was made of. For this He made something else called water, which also contained elements necessary for life. These, along with the elements in the soil, helped to make the plants and trees flourish.

Then He had to make life forms that were born free of the soil, and these had no root system to extract energy from the soil so they were made to eat the plants, fruits, and nuts from the trees and to absorb their energy. It was then that He realized that some control had to be made on the free life forms because they ate all the vegetation available and then starved to death. So He made life forms that fed on one another. Thus a balance was made and all life forms were able to flourish.

But unfortunately some of these life forms flourished more than the food supply that gave them energy, and many died. So it was very necessary that a proper balance be set up. He set in motion the proper balance and all the free animal life forms realized this balance and respected it.

Even his favorite animal He called Man respected this law of balance and practiced it with the other life forms. Man knew from experience that he had to live with nature and observe her rules if he wished to survive. He also learned to store food by drying it to use when food was not available.

As man progressed he made his life easier and in time made himself responsible for the other life forms. He is still in a learning stage about this and has much more to learn. Not all he does for his own benefit helps other life forms to survive. It is unfortunate that some other life forms have been lost forever due to his ignorance.

18. ARE YOU JUST YOU?

At this time, Born Many Times wanted to get into something really too deep for my feeble mind, and besides, I was concerned about how much more of this I could absorb. He felt that what he said was just commonplace information and was known to all people. Because he could recall past lives and the wisdom he acquired during these, he thought that all men were able to do the same. Well, I took great pains to make him understand that all men were not so gifted and most were completely ignorant about what he was talking about.

"I have told you about past civilizations and some famous people in history. I have tried to tell you about what makes you what you are and what you can accomplish. I will now have to tell you what makes you, you," he told me. He continued:

Since ancient times, man has looked outside of himself for answers about his existence. Now is the time to start looking within ourselves for these answers. Man has always looked for some thing or person to worship. Most of these things, for instance the sun which gives us life, do have an important role to play in human existence. Other planets and stars were made into gods by some peoples. Even some animals and plants were thought to have some great spiritual value to man and were worshiped. The Great Spirit, who is the same god that you worship today, and is known by different names in different cultures, is the center of all knowledge. Each living thing, whether human, animal or plant, is a part of god and so a part of this great knowledge.

We only have to learn how to receive this knowledge which is available to all living things. Of course, man, with his superior intelligence, is the chief benefactor of this knowledge, but as keeper of all other living things he must share this knowledge and put it to use if he is to survive.

When the white man came to our shores he found a people who had learned over centuries that they had to live with nature and abide by her laws. Now man is trying to make his own laws and to conquer nature. In this he is failing miserably. In fact, if no changes in his attitude are made soon, he will not be able to survive.

Let us take one item in this world of ours that is the most important to man's survival. It is the tree. Early man learned first to make tools of wood and rough shelters from its branches. He soon learned how to make clubs from wood. Later, he learned to make sharp projectiles and how to launch them.

Trees also gave him food such as nuts, fruits, sugar, and spices, as well as medicines. As he progressed in intelligence, man learned to use wood in many different ways for his benefit, too many to list here. He now knows that trees give him oxygen so he can live, as well as other chemicals that help him. Man in fact is sheltered, fed, allowed to float on water, live in and, in the end, is buried in wood from trees. But does man manage and care for the trees as he should?

Can you imagine a place without the benefit of wood? Well you are going to in the near future unless you begin to manage the forests better. This is just one important living thing that man will not be able to survive without. Without plant life man would perish. But man is the most intelligent animal living, and he will probably make the changes necessary, but not before he is in danger of extinction himself. Again, he can get help from the Great Spirit to help himself. He has to gain this knowledge from god by asking for it. Even though he has already been told what he is doing wrong and is aware of it, he will still get this help because god loves all things He has created. If we are receptive, we will be shown the way.

Why can we be so sure that we can and will get help? Because we are a part of the Great Spirit. He lives in all living things. He has given each of you life, a beautiful world to live in and other people to enjoy it with. One of the most important gifts he has given you is freedom of choice. This is to be used for the good of all living things. You are the only animal on the Earth that has this. Use it well, because so much life depends on it.

To do this you must learn to respect the dignity of all living things. Making animals appear like mankind is a deplorable thing to do. Making animals appear to have the intelligence of man is sinful. This includes taking animals and fish from their usual surroundings and putting them on display. The Great Spirit or god frowns on this practice. When it was said that he gave man dominion over animals he meant that we were to take care of them because they are His and they are part of Him just as you are.

So, when I asked the question, "Are you just you?", the answer is no, because you are part of many things. First, you are part of the Great Spirit and He is within you. You are also part of the Great Intelligence of the Universe because you have direct contact with It and as man, only you have this power. And you are born with an inquisitive mind that seeks answers to the many problems of life, and of everything that exists.

19. MYSTERIES

Now I was being still more confused by the information. I asked him why he jumped all over the place, from one lifetime to another. Talking of the distant past and of the times that I am existing in. There was a long silence, and then he told me that he moved from time to time because they were all one time. He said the past is also the present.

This confused me even more so I asked him, "Is there no future then?"

Again he was slow answering. "Naturally there is a future because time does not stand still, but the future is for those in the past and those who live in the present. Consider what time is in your present state. How do you measure this time?"

I told him it was measured by the Earth's movement around the sun and the spinning of the Earth.

"That is what I mean," *he said, and then he continued:*

Time is an invention of man where he happens to be existing. You measure your time by what is happening around you in your present existence. What if there is life such as yours living on another planet like Earth, but farther from a sun or larger than the sun; would it not measure time differently? If that Earth turned more slowly or faster, or if the sun rose in the south and set in the north, would not this make time different?

Do you think that the Great Spirit made only one Earth in all the universe? What if there are other Earths such as yours; would their time be calculated the same way as yours?

There is no such thing as time. There is no past because everything that happens does so now. It is your perspective that makes you aware of what you realize to be.

Astronomers have found stars that exploded millions of light years ago. This explosion is just reaching the eyes of scientist here on your Earth now. If you could go to the spot where the star had been you would find an empty void. But to you the star just disappeared now, when in fact it disappeared millions of your years ago. So it is all your perspective of time or your awareness of it.

Is there a future? No, because we have not made it yet. We have put into motion what the future will be, but it is not cast in stone. Many things can happen to change it, and this is where the Great Spirit and His giving man free will comes into play. How great was His intelligence when He gave man this power! What will happen to us is in our own hands. One man could not handle this great responsibility, so He gave it to all of us collectively so that we are all responsible for what happens in the future.

How can anyone deny that the Great Spirit is within all of us? To deny this is to deny life itself. Each one of us is unique and different. No two people are alike, and when you think of the billions of people on Earth today, you have a lot of different people. Who could create this if not the Great Spirit? Oh, there will always be the skeptics who claim it is just a natural occurrence. Well, I have a message for them, too! He made all the natural occurrences, and a lot more besides these, that no one person is yet aware of.

Your science today has made it possible to transplant organs from one body to another so they continue to live on in that body. Recently, a heart from a man who was an alcoholic killed in a motorcycle accident was transplanted into a young woman. This woman had never drunk an alcoholic beverage in her life. But after she recovered from the operation she had a desire to do so. Not only that, but she wanted a motorcycle, too.

Does this mean that the heart of the dead man could still influence the life of the young woman after a transplant? It appears that this is so. Scientists have now discovered that messages from the brain to other parts of the body are not transmitted through electric impulses but by body secretions. Perhaps this could explain this phenomenon.

In the future, perhaps they will be able to analyze these secretions and take some from one person's brain and put them into another, and then they could communicate without being in the vicinity of each other. They could perhaps even see or know what each other was doing. They may be able to transplant intelligence from one person to another who does not have that intelligence. This is almost like instant telepathy.

I leave you with this thought. The man known by you today as Jesus once said, "If you bring forth what is within you, what you bring forth will save you. If you do not bring forth what is within you, what you do not bring forth will destroy you."

20. BACK IN TIME

Born Many Times seemed to be apologetic in his manner the next time we met. He told me that he would try to remember other times that were important to the human race and what would affect them now. He said he would talk about a time in history so long ago that it would tax his memory to the extreme.

Man today believes that mankind began its existence on this Earth only a short time ago in comparison with the age of the Earth. This is not so. Man has been here for millions of years longer than is usually accepted. New evidence of this is being found by your scientists almost daily. Unfortunately, there are those in the scientific community who choose to disregard this evidence because they feel it would upset the accepted prevailing, though unproven, theories.

The scientists of your present world are guilty of collective, controlled thinking. Those who do not are considered mavericks or people who do not behave as they should. A good scientist is surely one who explores new ideas and solutions. Most present-day ones just accept the theories of their peers. The diggers and doers are the real scientists.

I will now speak of a time long ago when the Earth and its inhabitants were going through a transformation from early "caveman" to "intelligent beings". By this I mean there were men living on the Earth that were still in almost a primitive animal-like kind of existence.

There were other man-like beings who were becoming

culturally similar to present-day man. The caveman lived in small isolated groups in dense jungles. They appeared manlike in form but had some distinctly different appearances that one could see instantly. The most obvious was the hair which covered most of their bodies. They had sloping skulls with sunken eyes, flat noses and thick lips. Their teeth were even with prominent canine-like teeth much like meat-eating carnivores. They had short legs and powerful arms that hung from sloping shoulders, and they walked in a crouching position.

They lived in temporary structures of branches, overhanging rock ledges and caves. They wore animal skins and had primitive weapons—wooden spears and clubs. Meat was the mainstay of their diet, but they did eat vegetation when available. They knew the berries and nuts that they could consume safely. They did leave some rough artwork of animals and of their occupations. Their method of communication was by a primitive series of grunts, groans and gestures.

Meanwhile, in the same time period, there were humans that were further advanced in culture. These people stood straight, and, though they still had some body hair, they had different facial structures. The forehead was still sloping but their eyes were not sunken into the skull as were the others'. The nose was quite flat but the lower jaw was not as prominent. Their teeth were not as large or animal-like as the others'.

Standing and walking straight made them look taller and leaner. They still had muscular arms and legs. They lived in larger groups and had homes made of wood, stones and plant fibers. They had domesticated certain animals, so they had meat and skins for clothes. These people had more sophisticated weapons—spears with stone tips and bows and arrows.

They lived by the water and in the open countryside, going into the forest only to hunt animals and gather plants and fruit. They ate a lot of fish and cooked all their meat. They had a spoken language and were able to write this language using symbols.

These separate groups were constantly at war with each other. The more cultured group formed hunting parties to find and destroy the more primitive peoples' villages and families. The primitive people would raid some of the more isolated villages of the others.

It must be realized that though these people resembled each other, they were definitely of different species. The more cultured or human-like people eventually destroyed the others. There was some interbreeding, but the offspring were not able to reproduce.

Slowly, over the centuries, the people that were left developed into more recognizable humans by our standards. Their lives were complicated by widespread natural calamities such as floods, volcanoes, and earthquakes, and they were hunted by some larger and more fierce man-eating animals. But they did survive and became your ancestors.

Some of the hereditary traits of these people make up your lives today. The hair rising on your scalp and the back of your neck when you are afraid of something, for instance. Your ability to sense danger nearby. Your wanting to get back into a country setting or the forest to relax from the hurried life of the city. The feeling of communion with friends and relatives on special occasions, knowing there is safety in numbers. The wonder of the universe, and always being curious about what lies over the next hill.

Because of the unsatisfactory answers you receive from present-day religions, you seek out other means to answer your questions. Some of you go into the occult for answers while others enter metaphysical realms for understanding. Meditation is one practice some claim is just being discovered, when in fact it has been part of man's religion from the beginning of time. Ancient medical practices are being reborn, such as using natural herbs for healing and following a helpful diet. Now, there are numerous people accepting acupuncture to correct health problems. There are also faith healers that work on the soul and the energy systems of the body to make one well again.

It is impossible to list the many, many things that are now being recreated from the past to make people healthier and happier and their life more enjoyable. Most of them were practiced by your ancestors long ago.

A Neanderthal Hunter

The witch doctors of the primitive Africans and the shamans of your own natives knew many secrets that would be beneficial to you today. Do not forget that there are more than eighty different natural medicines available and used by you now that originated with the native peoples. One of the most widely used is aspirin, which was given to you by indigenous cultures.

History is full of stories about medicines used by the ancients. Even today you cannot duplicate the process of mummification of the body that the ancient Egyptians used in order to preserve the pharaohs. Skulls have been found that exhibit perforations resulting from operations on the brain. Many showed the bone healed over, proving that the operation had been successful—and you called them primitives!

21. A MAN NAMED YESHUA

There was a long period, about a month, when I was not in touch with Born Many Times. This was fine with me because I was busy with other things which had to do with living this lifetime. He was to tell me a story that I would rather not hear, because it disturbed my Christian upbringing immensely.

He asked me if I had heard of a man called Jesus Christ of Nazareth. I told him I had and had worshiped him in the past. He asked why only in the past, and I said the story of his life, as it is being told now, is not the truth and is only told today for the benefit of the church. I told him I had spent many long hours searching for the truth. He said, "Then you shall know it!" He began:

I had the fortunate experience of living one lifetime at the time in question when he was alive. I want you to understand that he was one of the greatest men that has ever lived in this world, but he is only one of such men. There have been others whose stories have not been told. I will tell you his story.

There lived a carpenter named Joseph who was married to a woman named Mary. They lived in a cave in a small village called Nazareth. Please understand that at that time a cave was one of the more desirable places to live. It had good strong walls that gave security from cold and rain. It also had only one entrance that was easily closed.

Most homes were made of mud bricks with brush and grass added. These were not as secure from rain and cold as was a cave, and they could be easily entered by anyone who wished to come in. They were usually small because of the supports used. Caves varied in size, but some were quite large, as Joseph's was.

Lumber was a very expensive commodity because most of it was imported from further north. It was generally used for furniture, but some of the larger buildings, such as synagogues and government buildings, used lumber extensively. Most of Joseph's work was on boats. In fact, Mary's brother owned a boat and made long voyages for trade on the Mediterranean.

At this time, the country was occupied by the Roman army under Pontius Pilate, who was in charge of everything. The Jewish king at the time was named Herod, but he was more or less just a vassal to Pilate and a very corrupt person.

Herod could do nothing without the permission of Pilate, but Pilate needed the cooperation of Herod. Judea, like Egypt, was needed by Rome for the large quantities of food it could supply. No countries on the Mediterranean were more necessary to conquer than these two for the food they could produce.

A decree issued by Herod at the insistence of Pilate ordered all citizens to return to where they were born to be registered. As Mary had been born in Bethlehem it was necessary for her to go there. She was pregnant, which made the trip more difficult for her. But the decree had to be obeyed, so Joseph and Mary made the trip from Nazareth.

It was a long and tiring trip with many people on the roads for the same reason. It was not easy getting accommodation on the road because of this, but it was still more difficult in Bethlehem.

They found that all the caravansaries were filled, and made their camp outdoors like many other people among the animals herded inside the walls of the caravansary.

A caravansary was a walled-in enclosure with rooms built into the wall and a water pool in the center. Each room was about eight feet square with three walls and the other side open to the center facing the pool. They had stone floors where each family slept on straw mats. Everyone could use the pool for washing clothes, bathing, and drinking. At night the animals were brought in, and they filled the space surrounding the pool.

Jesus of Nazareth

Contrary to what is believed today there was no such thing as an inn in this time or area. Inns were found only in Europe at a later period. There were no barns with mangers in this part of the world, either, at this time. Joseph and his wife found a corner near some people who felt sorry for Mary's plight. She was allowed to have a straw mattress on the floor along with the family. This was a raised floor above the animals.

Mary gave birth to their son during the early morning, and many people around them gave what help they could. The owner of the caravansary gave them a space to themselves when it became available, and during this time many people helped them. It was a good birth, and Mother and Son were healthy in spite of the circumstances. There were no wise men or exotic gifts as is now claimed.

When all was well for them to return home they did. They settled down to family life like everyone else in their village. No special treatment was given them that was better than anyone else received. Their son grew up as any boy of his time and circumstances. He attended the synagogue for religious teaching and for ceremonies, as all boys did.

Yeshua worked with his father in the carpenter shop, but it soon became apparent that he had no skills for this. He made many trips with his Uncle Joseph on his boat to far-off places. He went as far as England, where his uncle traded in tin because it was very scarce in Judea and surrounding counties. It was needed to make iron and bronze. It had become nearly as expensive as gold.

Yeshua finally decided he wanted to become a rabbi and was sent to the religious school to train. When he became a rabbi he found he was uncomfortable with the practice of sacrificing animals to god. It was impossible for the poorer people to buy animals for the sacrifice or to pay for special prayers. But there were always money lenders in front of the temple who would lend them money at a high interest rate.

These money lenders were actually working for the rabbis in the synagogue, and this meant the animals were sold at a profit. Worshipers borrowed money from the same source to pay for them. The dead animals were not given to the poor as was proper, but were sold again for a profit to meat dealers.

Yeshua made such a fuss about this practice that the synagogue leaders and high rabbis asked him to leave, which he did. He was still a devout Jewish rabbi and thought hard about his future. He decided that he should try to broaden his outlook on life with travel. He was still a young man in his early twenties when he left home.

He traveled to countries near his own and because of his interest in their beliefs and culture, he was welcomed. He went to Persia and Lebanon and spent a long time in Syria. He traveled most of the countries to the south, including Egypt, which he found to be most enlightening.

His greatest learning experience was in India where he soon learned yoga and became an expert in its practice. He learned to meditate and found out more about himself with this method than in any other way. He knew he must return to his homeland because his mission in life was to stop the corruption that was in the religion of his people.

He was also concerned that people were being told their god was a cruel and vengeful god. This made people fear Him, and to believe that death was a terrible ordeal. Instead, he preached about a tender, loving, and forgiving god who would forgive their sins if they would pray and ask for forgiveness. He taught them that all of mankind was equal in the sight of god.

When he returned to Judea, he was a lot more knowledgeable about how to proceed with his quest. He realized he could make no headway within the large city synagogues, but felt he could find some rabbis in smaller towns and villages that would listen, so he took to the countryside.

Wherever he went, he would gather together people to talk with. He preached the truth about the sacrifices and how they only helped the money lenders and the corrupt rabbis. In most cases he found a friendly audience, but there were some who disagreed with him and threatened to do him harm.

Fortunately, he found other men who felt as he did and followed his mission. One was a giant of a man called Peter who had been a fisherman. He had lost his boat to the money lenders when he could not meet his obligations. There were others who joined his group as he traveled, and soon there were twelve other men besides himself.

Not ever did he forget that he was a Jew and a rabbi. He offered prayers and shared knowledge wherever he preached or lectured. Many other rabbis agreed with what he said about the corruption of the leaders of their religion, and some refused to send their share of the money they had taken in to Jerusalem. Some would not allow the money lenders to practice near the synagogue.

These rabbis still had sacrifices, but they were done in a different way. They had the rabbi do the slaughtering in accordance with the laws of their Torah. This meant the animal was healthy and free of any disease. It had to be killed as humanely as possible. The owner of the animal being slaughtered remained the owner and could eat or sell its flesh as he desired. The rabbi was paid a fee for his service. This is the practice that evolved from the original sacrifices.

It was really a way to be sure the animal was properly bled after death, and that no animal or bird that had died a natural death, either from disease or old age, would be consumed by the people. It also meant that the animal was freshly killed because refrigeration was unknown in those days, and this was a very warm climate year round.

Because Yeshua was a very passionate and caring person, he did many good things when he had the opportunity. His studies in other countries had taught him many things that were not known in Judea. He knew that god was not some mysterious, austere person who lived in a place somewhere among the stars. He said many times, and I quote, "Our god lives in many mansions." This means that He lives in each one of us, and you are one of His mansions!

He also said at one time, and I quote again, "god has given each of us dominion over the animals and birds and all living things." This means that we must care for and protect living things and realize that they are part of us to be cherished as a gift from Him. Not many people accept this gift from god with conviction. We do many cruel and unjust things to nature's children.

It is impossible for one to be perfect, and god made allow-ances for this. Yeshua preached that you must first admit to yourself that you have done wrong and ask forgiveness, before you can feel forgiven. You do not have to have someone to intercede on your behalf, nor do you have to be inside a great building called a church to ask this forgiveness. You are your own church, and you must speak to the part of god that is within us all. Only then will you know that you have truly spoken to god.

Because Yeshua had been to other countries and spoken to and learned from these cultures, he became more wise. He became aware that he could be one with his Father, who is our Father, by doing and thinking with the age-old knowledge he had learned. Only by practicing what he preached did he become as holy as his teachers. Eventually he was able to do the remarkable things that are attributed to him.

When he finally returned to Judea, he found the same ceremonies being performed by the rabbis. The people were still bringing live animals to be sacrificed, and the poor had to borrow from the money lenders to get animals for the sacrifices.

Yeshua traveled the countryside teaching, as a rabbi was required to do. He was forbidden to go to Jerusalem because of his campaign against sacrifices.

Yeshua did comfort and heal the sick, as has been told, and he said all men could do this. There was never another with more love and compassion than he for his fellow humans and all living things. He was sincere in all he did for people's benefit. He told people about a loving and forgiving god, very different from the god they were told about in the synagogues.

Not everyone believed in Yeshua's message. Instead, they stood by what they had learned from their own rabbis. Like many religious people, they did not take too kindly to new thoughts or ideas about their beliefs. Some acted toward him and his group with savage indignation. In contempt, his group were called the unemployed fishermen. This was somewhat true, because many of them, like Peter, had lost their boats and gear to the money lenders at the synagogues and could no longer ply their trade.

In the meantime, Yeshua's fight against the money lenders was having the desired effect. More and more people would not participate in the sacrifices, and this meant that the revenues for the temples were down.

Due to the many complaints he was receiving, Herod asked Pilate to do something about this troublesome rabbi. Pilate told him that it was his own problem, and to take care of it in his own way.

Yeshua was therefore summoned to Jerusalem to answer charges brought against him. When he arrived, he went to a safe haven where he could pray and meditate.

When Yeshua was finally brought before him, Pilate decided that this man had broken no laws of the Romans, so he was turned over to the court of Herod's rabbis to be judged. It was decided that he would be put on the cross like every criminal of that time.

But the wife of Pilate had heard Yeshua preach and realized that he was a good man who did not deserve such harsh treatment. She prevailed upon her husband to do something to save him.

It was therefore decided that Yeshua would fake death, and, being a master in the practice of yoga, this was easy for him to do. He would then be taken to his uncle's boat and sail to southern France. This place was chosen because freedom was given to everyone there.

After the evening meal which he had with his friends, Yeshua was taken prisoner. No one informed on him about his whereabouts. The authorities were well aware where he was. He was taken before the court and sentenced. The next morning he was put on the cross. This meant he was tied to the cross. He was never nailed there. Iron and steel were much too scarce and expensive to waste on criminals.

Contrary to what is believed, Yeshua never said he thirsted. Nor did he ask god why He had forsaken him. The only things he said were words of comfort and hope to the other unfortunate prisoners hanging on the crosses around him. He told them that god had forgiven their sins and was making a place in His kingdom for their souls because He loved them. Never did he criticize those who tormented him or who had placed him where he was. He forgave them all.

As had been previously arranged, he went into a death state about three hours after being hung on the cross. Ordinarily, a man would hang on the cross for at least three days before he expired. But Pilate wished this man no more discomfort than necessary, because he realized that indeed this was a great man. Who else under such torture would concern himself about others before himself?

Yeshua was taken away to a tomb that was prepared for him and there he was revived and given new clothes. He was given permission to speak with Peter to let him know he survived. He then was quietly taken to his uncle's boat and they set sail for France. Later his mother and wife, both named Mary, were to join him there.

Yeshua lived for many years among the people in France and farmed as they did. Eventually they learned of his background and he was accepted as a good man. He continued to help and teach the people and they grew to love and respect him. He left many offspring who would in later years show intelligence, inspiration, love, and hope to the people. But none had the spiritual knowledge he had and above all the love and dignity he gave to people.

Was he one of a kind? Certainly not. There have been numerous men and women who have given the same spiritual message and shown goodness to others.

Other religions have had their spokesmen with a similar message. Every one of these teachings has been manipulated to serve the religions' present-day hierarchy. The churches have re-written the history of this man to make a business of his works so that it can become rich and powerful and manipulate his followers.

It is ironic that he gave himself up to stop that which has now become prevalent. If you really believe in this great man you will understand what they do in his name today is not what he intended or taught.

To say that he died for your sins is unbelievable. He appeared to die because the corruption in the temples gave him great concern for his god and his people. To say that all people are born in sin is ridiculous. He never said that. Society makes rules for your behavior so everyone can live together in peace, security, and harmony. It has nothing to do with god or religion. god made His rules which are in nature and we must obey them to survive. The only punishment you shall ever receive is the damage you have inflicted on yourself.

I have explained in previous talks with you that each living thing has a small part of god within them. This god Energy stays with all as long as they live. But this same god Energy can be expanded upon within a person by constant learning and putting into practice this new knowledge for the good of his fellow man. Yeshua had expanded his god Energy beyond what can be expected by any man.

Furthermore, he put to good use this knowledge specifically for the good of all men. But I repeat he was not the only person to do this. Another thing that I should bring to your attention is that rabbis were forbidden to have any hair on their faces at the time of Yeshua, so therefore any pictures showing him with hair on his face are not as he looked at all.

22. ANOTHER TIME, ANOTHER PLACE

After this long talk about Yeshua, Born Many Times was absent for almost three months. I had so much to digest that I really appreciated his being away. Finally he appeared to me and asked if I was ready to work again. This time he told me we would discuss the lost world of Atlantis. He knew that present-day opinion was divided as to whether it ever existed. He said that it had, and that he was going to tell me about it.

I myself was a firm believer that it had existed as well as other ancient populations that now are gone. Today scientists and archae-ologists will not believe anything that differs from the status quo. They have a mind-set that is hard to crack. Many are creationists and must only believe what they have learned in academic circles. At times I almost think that some of them still believe the world is flat. He continued:

The continent of Atlantis had Europe and Africa on one side and North America on the other. It was separated from each by salt water seas. Some refer to it as an island, but it was too vast an area for that. The temperature ranged from cool in the north to warm in the south. It could become extremely cold in the north and extremely hot in the south, but was temperate between these areas.

Because of this, the people could grow a wide variety of fruits and vegetables. They had a large population and of these many were immigrants from surrounding countries. The expanse of water between them and their neighbors was not great and could easily be managed by the boats they had. In fact, they had a very lucrative trading arrangement with their neighbors.

This trade was mostly with the countries to their east because those to their west were not developed to any extent and had sparse populations made up of isolated tribes. The Atlantean people did a lot of mining because the land had a large mineral content. Fish and game were easy to come by, and there were good trade relations with the tribes for these products. These tribes were not as civilized as the Atlanteans, who gave them special treatment to help them.

Many of the Atlanteans explored the area to their west to seek out different people to educate and help. They instructed them in how to build sturdier buildings and how to farm to get more yield. They showed them how to measure time and the seasons to make them more productive. Some they taught how to write and to study the night sky and learn astronomy. They also taught them the skills to build pyramids, libraries, observatories, and storage buildings.

Many Atlanteans had gone to the east and in some countries had taught as they had in the west. They were superb sailors and explored most of the world. Their world then was much different than your present world. The poles were not where they are now. They understood the things that affected climate and ocean and wind currents. They had more accurate star maps than we have today.

The ocean that surrounded Atlantis was constantly moving. It flowed north on the west side and south on the east. This meant that their continent was warmer on the west coast than on the east. They did their crop planting to take advantage of this. This meant that they were harvesting crops all year and so were well fed. They had transportation methods that moved the food to places where there was none. They had animals that pulled wheeled vehicles along stone-paved roads.

Because of their seafaring abilities, they had maps that were more accurate than some you have made today. When scientists compare these maps with those of the present time, they are amazed at the Earth changes that have taken place since this period. It makes one wonder how they obtained this information when others in the same time and place did not have it. If you cannot believe in Atlantis then you will not believe where this information came from.

I am aware that what I say will shock some of your readers, but common sense should make them believe. The information they had received came from beings from another planet!! In other words, they were aliens or, as some describe them, extra-terrestrial beings. It really does not matter what you call them. They exist, and sooner or later humankind must accept this. I cannot understand how earthly beings are so ignorant or arrogant as to think that the Almighty god by whatever name you know Him would put life only in one place in this vast universe.

I am amazed that with such compelling evidence available now people still reject this truth. There are more than a million galaxies in the universe that are the same as yours, and this is a minimal guess. They can and do support life.

You would accept it with no problem if you could go to one and see for yourselves, but the distances are too great for your technology. But that does not mean that other intelligent beings cannot do it. It does not mean that they have to look like you. Maybe they do not contact you because you are too unstable to accept them.

Nonetheless, they had contacted the Atlanteans and this is why Atlantis was so much more advanced than were other nations of those times. They told the Mayans, Olmecs and Toltecs what they had learned from the Atlanteans.

Why would these people make huge pictures on the ground that are not discernable except from a great height? Why were there pictures created by natives north of Blyth, California, that can only be seen from the air?

How did ancient mariners get such accurate maps of the oceans and landmasses? There were no trained geographers in ancient times. How could they have mapped the skies so accurately without telescopes or any kind of method to enlarge their view? How could they possess a calender more accurate than the ones used in later times? How could they know that some planets in your galaxies had moons circling them when they had no way to even see the planets clearly?

It boggles the mind that the scientists in your time deny that extraterrestrials have been and are visiting your planet even today. Are they afraid that humankind will not be able to cope if they know the truth? Is humankind's faith in god and the universe so shallow? Is their intelligence to be bound by what they have been allowed to know and see? What a pity! There is so much to be learned, and humankind has not even begun to learn it.

Humankind has learned things like how to travel your Earth in high speed aircraft, boats, trains, and automobiles. They have been able to transport images by air using radio waves. They have been able to mass produce the necessities of life. There have been great strides in medicine. But they have not—and this is most important—been able to live without the fear of death, even though it is inevitable for all living things.

You have still not learned that there is no such thing. When will you learn that death is just another form of consciousness? If and when humankind finally makes contact with extraterrestrials, this will be the most important thing they will learn. They will know that life never ends. Think about it. If, as you have been told, you are part of god and He created you, do you think that He would kill Himself by killing you? Does this make sense to you?

It is amazing that any intelligent being cannot realize this truth. In present-day religion, you are told that if you behave you will go into the kingdom of heaven. Heaven is pictured as the perfect place, and you will live there happily for all eternity. If this is so, why do not the people who preach this go there now? Why waste time talking about it if it is so great? Because they are not too sure it exists themselves. Even their faith is found wanting. These very people do not want to face death. The Atlanteans were assured that death was not the end of life. They knew there were other planes of consciousness made available to them depending on how much they had progressed and become aware in their present lifetimes. This understanding was available for them, then, and still is today in your time. Humankind must develop their sense of place and being within the whole Universe.

The Atlanteans were taught to build a building in a special way such as in a pyramid shape aligned with certain planets in the sky. By using exact measurements, this gave them a source of power. They could use this power to charge instruments to defy the Earth's gravity. With it they could lift stones weighing many tons as though they were weightless. This is how they built the pyramids in Egypt and in Central America.

The stones used in the Coral Garden at Homestead south of Miami, Florida, by Edward Leedskalnin were moved in this way by a very frail man without any help from others. Other structures in North America built by native peoples used the same technology.

Some of these types of stone structures will be found soon on other planets in your own galaxies. The controversial mile-long face on Mars is one of these. Some of these structures have already been seen and observed by your present-day scientists, but this information has not been disclosed to the general public. Why is it that civilizations before yours were aware of these things and yours is not? There are references to such phenomena in the Bible and other religious literature. Other historical documents mention them as well. Still, your academics only speculate about them. They seem not to want to accept anything that doesn't fit currently accepted theories.

The Atlanteans knew more about this technology than they do. Being in close contact with extraterrestrials made them more knowledgeable about this. They knew many other things that they had learned by close observation of the heavenly bodies. They had methods of examining the stars and galaxies that are still beyond your scope, even today. Why do so many of the structures of ancient humankind resemble the location of star clusters seen by the naked eye?

It is well known that the pyramids of Giza and the pyramids of Mexico are exactly located to resemble, or are oriented toward, certain star clusters. This was no accident. Was there some powerful reason for doing this? Of course there was. The people who caused these colossal buildings to be erected previously came from these star groups. But why they had these structures copy their part of the universe is not known.

23. UNKNOWN POWER SOURCE

Born Many Times seemed, as we would say, to be on a roll. His information was coming in an enthusiastic manner. It was all I could do to keep up with what he was giving and he showed some annoyance with me. He ignored my attempts to slow him down and continued as though I didn't exist.

In ancient times things were very different than they are now. Humankind knew that the sun gave off tremendous amounts of energy. This was trapped by the Earth, and most was absorbed, though some bounced off. They also knew that the Earth was itself a giant dynamo with a molten core that turned within the Earth's crust and so created energy, too.

These energies were too strong to remain within the Earth and, like water, sought an easy way to escape. If they had not, the Earth would have exploded with a tremendous force. Fortunately the Earth's crust has cracks that let surplus energy escape. These places where the energy escapes are called power spots and are known to sensitive people even today. Most primitive peoples were quite conscious of these places and used them for many purposes.

On these power spots the people were told to build the pyramids. If you really examine the pyramids they look like inverted funnels. This is what they are. They funnel the energy escaping from the Earth's core into a small point on the top of the pyramid.

This makes a tremendous energy point that can charge anything within the pyramid. If a certain tool were left there to be charged it could, by touching something, make it defy gravity. Naturally the extraterrestrials brought with them these gravity-defying tools which were used to build the first pyramid.

In this way they could lift the huge stones that were required to build pyramids and other colossal structures. If enough of these were placed in a confined space, the container would become completely gravity-free. Then, if one were to supply some type of energy to make the gravity-free container move, it could travel anywhere, even into space. This is where the UFO's get their power and ability to move anywhere in space.

It is surprising that your scientists have not become aware of this untapped power. Surely they could have learned from the man who built the Coral gardens in the Florida peninsula. In his workshop were found home-made generators using old wheel castings. He called the power magnetic, but it was on a power point that he had his garden and developed his anti-gravity tools.

I find it amazing that the ancient Chinese people had ley lines which they knew were power points. Native Americans, Mayans, Aztecs, Incas, and Amazons knew, and some of them still know, about power points, while modern scientists do not. They persist in using fossil fuel to make energy when there is a source available that is pollution-free. Someday soon they are going to make the world uninhabitable with their use of these fuels.

The signs are there, but are ignored, mainly because of money and wealth.

There can be nothing as cheap as energy from the sun unless someone finds a way to charge you for it, and they probably will. When the oil supply runs out, then science will find an alternative. To be fair, they are doing some work on it but not nearly aggressively enough and not in the right direction.

They have found a way to use the Earth's spin on its axis to propel rockets out of the Earth's gravity and to use the same methods to trap the spacecraft back into the Earth's pull upon its return. This is a beginning.

24. MORE ON ATLANTIS

Born Many Times had previously mentioned the lost continent of Atlantis. Many do not believe that it existed, but they are wrong. There is just too much evidence to suggest otherwise. Born Many Times is adamant that there was such a place and he brought up the topic again:

I have mentioned Atlantis and the people that lived there but have not explained why it disappeared so many years ago. This had nothing to do with their remarkable science, but because of sudden Earth changes that were inevitable. They knew these changes were coming and were powerless to do anything to change them.

Now, in your time, scientists know about tectonic plates and fractures. They have studied earthquakes and volcanoes. But even with their new knowledge, they still cannot predict with any positive certainty when these will happen. The Atlanteans did. They knew there were going to be great movements of the plates and they prepared for it as best they could. But they didn't know the extent of the damage they were facing.

Little did they realize that their continent would move to the west and go under the North American continent where it is today. They had many earthquakes, volcanoes and huge tidal waves just before their continent slipped under the one to their west.

First, they knew a wide crevice had opened in the east under the water the length of their whole continent. They could see that the land to their east was getting further away.

In the west, the land was coming closer and their own land was sinking into the ocean. Can you imagine such a catastrophe? Can you understand the fear and anguish of the people? Some rushed to the east to try to save themselves, but this area was being engulfed in huge tidal waves. The continent now called Africa existed many millennia before it had been pushed up and under the southern parts of Europe and created the Pyrenees mountains. Now that same continent was moving to the south again, creating a new sea now called the Mediterranean.

In the west, the two long strips of land separated by another shallow sea were being pushed up by the Atlantean continent which was sliding under it. This drained the shallow sea and joined the two long strips of land into one big continent now known as North America. These two long strips of land were joined and now contained high mountain ranges.

Eventually all that was left of Atlantis were a few islands in the west now known as the Caribbean Islands and a few to the east that are known today as the Canary Islands. Most of the landmass of Atlantis was under the North American continent. It is hard to imagine the immensity of this terrible catastrophe. This Earth change killed many thousands of people. It has taken thousands of years for humankind to recover enough to rebuild a significant culture again.

The first catastrophe to hit Atlantis was the splitting up of the continent, with the larger part sliding under North America and the smaller part going under Africa, resulting in Africa moving to the south and slightly east. This created the Mediterranean Sea. Greenland was also affected by being forced to the north and east.

After the Atlantean survivors had rebuilt their lives and new cities on the islands, they were confronted by the glacial period. Many of the people had emigrated to the west and east, taking their knowledge with them. These emigrants were responsible for the great pyramids and other structures in Egypt and South America being built. The Atlanteans also passed on to other people their knowledge of agriculture.

When the glacial period arrived, they were not directly affected for a long time, except that the ocean water level dropped and exposed more land. The temperature became quite a bit cooler but was not unlivable. The glacial period took more than five thousand years to form, yet it disappeared in less then three thousand.

The inhabitants of the islands began to notice the change in temperature and the water level beginning to rise. It eventually covered the cities they had constructed near the shorelines. These Earth changes then became dramatic. On the North American continent, there had been a shallow ocean before the Earth plate moved and brought most of it above water. Here, the bulk of the ice lay a mile thick in height.

Now, as the ice melted, it left an accumulation of soil it had moved down from farther north. As the ice melted, the water flowed south adding to the erosion and making the now-exposed central plane flat, fertile prairie land. Many of the descendants of the original survivors of Atlantis moved into this area. These people now lived on the east side and further to the south on the upraised continent.

Most of the native peoples of East, North, and South America were descendants of the Atlanteans. Only those in the Northwest entered over the land bridge linked to the Orient. Many of the natives in the Southwest came from over the Pacific ocean and interbred with the people who had settled in the east. Many sites have been found in recent years that predate the existence of the last ice age and the much-reported land bridge. This proves beyond a doubt that there were people living on the North American continent long before this land bridge existed.

Earth changes have hidden and in some cases buried past civilizations that are now unknown because of lack of evidence that they ever existed. This is not the case with Atlantis because there is ample evidence of its existence still to be found off Bimini in the Bahamas.

I worked with Dr. Norman Emerson, a noted Canadian archaeologist, until his death in 1978. We had done research projects in many parts of the world. One of these involved the Association for Research and Enlightenment and the Edgar Cayce Foundation. We worked with them in Egypt, Israel, and Iran. I met and became friends with Hugh Lynn Cayce, the son of Edgar Cayce, the renowned psychic known as "The Sleeping Prophet."

Once, when we were in Dr. Emerson's study in his home near Unionville, Ontario, he showed me some small pebbles that he had received from Hugh Lynn. He asked me to look at them and tell him what I could about them. He did not tell me anything about them nor where they were found. I studied the pebbles for quite a long time and told Emerson they were very cold and this to me meant that they were from a very old site. I finally told Dr. Emerson that they were connected to a very old civilization called Atlantis and that they had come from present-day Bimini. This is an island of the Bahamas.

Emerson then verified that they were indeed from Bimini and had been sent to him by Hugh Lynn Cayce. During the half hour or so of the experiment the room had become very cold, and in fact Emerson and I were both trembling. We went upstairs to the living room and our wives made us hot coffee to warm us up. The next morning we discovered that certain small plants in his study had become frost-bitten. In no way was the temperature cold enough to do this. Dr. Emerson attributed this to the fact that I had used the heat energy from the room to take me so far back in time.

This was my first involvement with Atlantis. I did no further research on it until the Spring of 1997, when I was asked by two gentlemen to go to Bimini and do some research there. Because of my own curiosity I agreed to go. My wife Charlotte was asked to accompany me and when she agreed I was delighted, because she had a keen interest in Atlantis too.

We flew to Miami and took a seaplane to Bimini. On our arrival there, we were met by our hostess who was the owner of the apartment complex where we were to stay. Bimini is a very small island, almost horseshoe-shaped. It has tropical vegetation, mangrove trees being the most visible. We learned that no food is grown on the island. All of it is brought in either from Miami or Nassau.

Fishing is the main industry here, followed by tourism. The American author Ernest Hemingway spent a lot of time here fishing *and writing. It is a friendly, quiet place. The highest population density is along a sand spit about five miles long. The northeast shore is unoccupied. Bimini is really made up of three separate sections surrounding an ancient volcano top. The crater that the island surrounds is very shallow with a sand bottom.*

This was originally an Atlantis outpost, used by the Atlanteans for their trading boats to gather supplies and water and to repair their ships. The principal city of Alantis was to the east and further south. When the original problem began, Atlantis was in Mid-Atlantic ocean. After much of it had slid beneath the North American continent, the only remaining islands were those in the Caribbean and the Canaries.

Most of the inhabitants had migrated to the continent to the west though some went to the east. These were the people whose skills made it possible for the pyramids of Egypt and South America to be built. Because of catastrophic Earth changes most of these skills became lost.

Many of the people of what is now Bimini were lost to tidal waves and earthquakes. Those that survived began to rebuild their civilization.

But again, as the ice age ended, the rising water engulfed their cities, and again they had to abandon the island when it became uninhabitable.

My research started at the Atlantis wall, which is clearly visible from a boat above it. I knew it had been built by human hands many centuries before. To know and to prove this are very different things. But there is some proof. A few years ago some investigators vacuumed the sand away from under the huge stones and discovered they were sitting on red granite pegs. Mother nature does not do this.

In Miami there are jetties that were installed using red granite boulders taken by barge from under the water near Bimini. It has been reported that some of these stones show holes with six sides drilled through them. Some of these holes do not go straight through the stone, but take fairly sharp turns. I have never heard of a modern drill that can make holes with six points and that can go in any direction but straight. Other holes show that it was drilled with some tool that left the edges burned smooth.

Most of these stones showed they have been worked with human hands. Further, this type of stone is not native to Bimini. The closest supply is in Georgia, USA. Yet there is still the same amount of red granite left near Bimini that was taken away to Miami.

It has also been reported that residue of a glue found on the granite is harder than the granite itself. This same type of glue has been found at other ancient sites where stone was piled together. Other underwater structures are known to exist in the area and other pieces of marble worked by man have been found.

Surprisingly, scientists avoid any research in this area. It is much like their lack of interest in the artifacts given Father Crespi by the Indians in Ecuador. I have been there and handled these artifacts. I found them to be very old indeed. Do our scientists fear that new information will make them rethink history and their cherished theories? I think so.

There is so much evidence available today to make one realize that Atlantis did indeed exist. This evidence is not refutable. Even if just the writings from historical documents were taken into account, they would realize this. There sits something that would help explain the existence of ancient man and his environment, and it is totally ignored.

25. BEGINNING WITH PROPHECIES

I was out of touch with Born Many Times when I went on the trip to Bimini and did my research there. I then wrote the preceding. When we were finally able to make contact, I asked him if he could tell me what was going to happen in the future, to the world, to people and about coming Earth changes. I told him anything he could forecast would be appreciated. He took a long time to answer and finally he told me that he hesitated to forecast the future for the same reason that I did. Man can change his future, so therefore mankind has not really made his future yet.

With all the literature being presented today about the coming millennium and the Earth changes being forecast, I wondered if the future was worth learning about. How so many authors can know and write about it is amazing to me. It is interesting that because a comet streaks across the sky or a new century begins there are said to be so many things that are going to happen to humankind. Do these things really influence what is about to happen? Or is it just that so much energy is put into forecasting it that it will come to pass? We will see very soon how accurate these prophecies are.

I had to agree with Born Many Times because I never did try to tell anyone their future. I learned that the minute you say it, it can be changed. I always believed that there are exceptions, because of events coming about that will solidify certain predictions. So I asked him to tell me those things that are not changeable. He scolded me and told me all things are changeable. But he did say that he would think it over and contact me later.

And later he did contact me and agreed to tell me what the future of things were shaping up to be, though the moment he said them, he repeated again that things can be changed.

First of all he wanted to talk about the environment, and I agreed that this was a worthy subject and he continued.

Humankind looks at the environment like it is something separate from itself. How can they be so blind? They *are* the environment. They clutter up the landscape more than any other living thing. Why do they try to separate themselves from it? Whether they like it or not, they are part of this Earth and of everything in it. If they destroy it, they destroy themselves, and they are busy doing this right now.

Eventually, when they have all but destroyed themselves and the world, they will realize that there must be a real world order that can control their foolishness. Humankind must come to realize that any time a tree is cut down, the world has that much less oxygen. With the world's population out of control, they need every bit of oxygen that can be produced for them.

Those whose job it will be to take care of the environment will have to have the power to do so. Everyone in the world must be made to obey the decisions of this body, which must be appointed by the world order. Punishment needs to be severe enough to make everyone obey the law. These laws must be put into place to protect everybody. There would be no unemployment anywhere in the world if people were put to work now to repair the damage done so far. Payment may be high, but a dead world is an awful price to pay, too, and believe me, that is the final price.

Every time you do damage you are not just destroying your world, but that of your children, grandchildren, and on and on. Are future generations not worth saving?

Removing the forests is not the only environmental problem facing mankind now and in the future. But if you do not start now, the damage can become irreversible. Man pollutes the air with chemicals that change to acid rain. This kills the trees and plants that make the oxygen necessary for life to exist, so man is killing himself. As the world population increases, there is more pollution and so less oxygen to share.

What I have said above ought to scare people into action, but knowing humankind it will not. Each of you think that the other person will do it, so why bother? Nor do you see what you can do that will make a difference. That is why there must be a world body with real power to oversee the environment. It must be no longer possible for one country to destroy forest land for short-time gain.

For the sake of mankind, there will have to be a real authority that will be independent of ethical, religious, national, and business interests. It will be in place for the sole good of all life forms that inhabit this Earth. It may be a tall order to create this authority, but one that is absolutely necessary.

When humankind was made up of isolated groups, they were no danger to each other because of their small numbers. Even when they had joined into areas for their common good, they were still able to act independently. Over time, areas all over this world had different groups of people of different colors, races, customs, and governments.

As time went on, these different groups engaged in warfare to try to dominate the other, or to seize that which the other had. This warfare created a ruination of life to all living things. But eventually there came to be only one dominant group. They tried to become all things to all people, but because of ethical and religious differences and prejudices, they failed.

In the meantime, there were more people needing more things, and they eventually used up what was available. So it came about that humankind was now unable to support the number of people that existed, so some had to go. Fortunately, now this decision will not be up to humankind to make. Mother nature will make it for them.

In a cold, abstract way, this is what can happen. But we must not forget the intelligence of humankind. Hopefully they will find a solution and this will be in a world order as described above. There can no longer be the extravagance of individual actions. The world is too finely balanced for one group to control or use the actions and resources of everyone else as it feels fit. There must be one recognized body of authority whether we like it or not.

There is existing today in your time many different groups vying to become prominent among you. Not just between countries and ethnic groups, but even between the really only difference between humans and that is the genders. Man and woman are becoming hostile to each other because one wishes to remain dominant and the other to become equal. It has now become common for them to find life mates of the same sex, although it will be argued this is not the reason.

I have tried to give you background on your only home, the Earth, on how it will react and what will happen if things continue as they are and what it will take to save it.

26. NEW PROPHECIES

I was not happy with what Born Many Times had predicted for our future and wanted to know about things that would happen in the coming millennium. I asked him to try to stay closer to my time and space, and he said he had to say what he did. He wanted us to know where we are heading if we keep on doing what we are doing. He promised to try to keep within our bounds.

There are things going on now that are obvious to those who take the most critical view. The ocean currents are changing, bringing climatic changes that are sometimes violent. The torrential rainstorms and flooding are causing havoc in many places. The loss of fish in places where they were abundant a few years ago is another clue to these changes. A lot of this can be attributed to over-fishing and mismanagement. But when there is so much flooding in areas every year, it must tell another story.

Your scientists keep complaining that the Earth is warming up because of the ozone layer becoming weak from pollution. This is just one reason. The ozone layer is being rejuvenated constantly and will correct itself when needed. But there is another reason. Beginning in this coming millennium, there will be many Earth changes. So many you cannot believe it now.

There will be more earthquakes where none have occurred before. Volcanoes will become active again. There will be more hurricanes and tornadoes. The world will become a more violent place weatherwise. The ice caps will melt, causing flooding of the land and of cities close to the ocean shoreline.

There will be food shortages because of climate changes. Fresh water will become scarce because of the pollution caused by these changes.

There will be more and deadlier diseases. There will be shortages of everything you use and need now. This will cause mankind to turn on itself. There will be wars and destruction among you. Race, religion, and nationality will no longer exist, because survival will be the consuming activity among people.

Humankind will eventually realize that all this is the forerunner of the next ice age, which will take about three thousand years to form, then last ten thousand years. After this, the ice will begin to melt and the human race will again be able to re-establish itself.

This is not to say the continents will remain the same as they are. Nor will the North and South poles be in the same position. After such an Earth change, the poles will have to rebalance themselves. The time to make a complete turn on its axis will be slightly slower, and this will make big changes in atmospheric pressures and temperatures. The ice caps by the poles will be much larger. New landmasses will be formed and ocean currents will change direction.

This will take many centuries to occur, and hopefully humankind will be able to adapt to their new surroundings. All life on Earth has gone through this many times before, so it will be no different this time. It will just be a long, painful process. The previous ice age reduced humankind to a near animal existence, so this will likely be no different. There will be none of the things that you take for granted today, such as means of transportation, machines to do everything but think for you, and the medical miracles that exist now.

Humankind will have to be satisfied with just the tools to survive in a new world that is completely foreign to them. Next to food and lodging, the family will be the most important unit. It gives security and safety in such an environment. What I have described will take thousands of years to come about, but there are more immediate concerns.

How to avoid many of the things I prophesied is most

important, and only by concentrated effort now will human-kind avoid the catastrophes that I am telling you can happen. They are not all under your control, but those that are should be given close attention.

27. IMMEDIATE PROPHECIES

Again I asked Born Many Times to get to the prophecies that will affect me and my future and others here now. He said he would but wanted me to know that history repeats and repeats itself, so I should not be too concerned about the near future. He said that all individuals living now will have to face the end of their cycle of life here in this plane of consciousness, although knowing this does not make them want to get to the end before their time. So the changes in the future should not make us want to get to them before their time.

I will try to take each change in separate chapters so they will be easier to understand. The first will be in medicine. As your medical researchers now realize, bacteria and germs can mutate so quickly that wonder drugs cannot keep up with them and are becoming ineffective. Bacteria seem to have the ability to make the drug work for them rather than against them. In other words, the more you use a drug the stronger the bacteria becomes.

Many different bacteria live within our bodies that were put there by our mothers before we were even born. As we put food into our bodies, other bacteria gain entrance. The human body can keep these bacteria in check naturally until something happens to make them dangerous to us. So it seems the simplest solution to having good health is to keep these bacteria dormant. And with a little help along the way, the body does this quite well. There are a few simple ways where you, the owner of this wondrous machine, can help.

First of all, you are the owner of this body and it is the only one you will have in this world. So it is up to you to take care of it. Do not let anyone else take control of it, whether it be a doctor, lawyer, or a politician. Only you should be in charge. You need to realize that what you put into your body makes all the difference in whether you are healthy or not. Moderation is the key.

Good, wholesome food is the best source of good health. But today your food is laced with chemicals that cause problems. It is virtually impossible to avoid all the chemicals in your food. But by trying, one can avoid a lot of it. Many stores are featuring organic food. It is a little more expensive, but that would change if the demand were there. Growing your own food is the best answer, and in that way you get the food while it still has some life in it. This is probably not possible for most of you.

Vitamin and mineral additives to your diet are helpful, but this can be carried too far. If you were to take all the vitamins and minerals that are supposed to be necessary for your health, you wouldn't have room in your body for them. Use only what you require. So be selective and read up on them to know which you can depend on and need. There are many good books available to help you.

Some doctors can be of help to you. Many are not. Most older people need some vitamins to help them as they grow older, and these are easy to come by. There are naturopaths who do good work and give excellent advice on supplements. It is easier to stay well than become sick. Alternative medicine will become more popular in the future.

Medical doctors and surgeons are the backbone of your health system and well being. They do miraculous things to keep you healthy. But in the near future people will not see a doctor. There will be electronic scans that will pinpoint any defect in your body and will transfer that data to an analyzer that will immediately recommend proper treatment. You will not have any use for the medical practitioners as you know them today. The human element will be gone, along with misdiagnosed ailments and the need for useless operations and medication.

This would be possible today with the equipment available, but there is a resistance by the medical establishment that prevents their use. The huge cost of the present system makes it obsolete and unnecessary. There will, of course, still be a need for highly trained surgeons. They will use more technical and sophisticated equipment that will make their job easier and will prevent human error. Mini-surgery will become more common with this equipment. Hospital stays will be minimal.

There will be less illness because prevention will be used more than now. There will be more natural ways to cure people. Man-made chemicals will become obsolete in years to come. There are no man-made medications that cannot be found in natural plants and substances. There will be a way found to make use of the common ground and common good that exists between nature and man.

28. NEWER PROPHECIES

As I listened to Born Many Times, I had a real interest in today's medical problems of high cost for hospitals and treatment. I had investigated the natural medicine that he agreed with. He had given an account of a way to stop the high cost with electronic medical scans and surgery, less invasive operations, and less recuperating time. But with it all, he continually stressed prevention, prevention, prevention. Keep healthy naturally. Involve yourself with healthy activities.

I appreciated what he had said and now wanted to hear more about the future. He said he would tell me about how we would live and where and why. He cautioned that a lot of toes would likely be stepped on, but he didn't care, because they would have a hard time finding his toes. I was surprised that he did have a sense of humor after all.

People of your time and space are no different than people from any part of your history. You want a home that is secure and warm and a place to live and raise your family. In your time, your lifestyle dictates the type of accommodation you desire. The more money you have the more elaborate and more desirable the location you choose. This tends to be a class distinction thing.

People with more moderate means can still enjoy living in an area with those of the same means as well as those with greater means.

Even the poorest people find happiness and contentment living among people who have the same living standard as they do. Many spend their whole lifetimes striving to raise their standards of living so they can live in the best neighborhood with what they consider to be the best people. What a waste of life!

Why is real estate so expensive and what is the result? Greed is the most important reason. The person who owns property wants as much as he can get for it. The broker selling the property wants as much commission as he can get. The politicians want as much taxes as they can get. So it goes on. Other reasons are apparent. Supply and demand and good location can influence the price. The result is that many younger couples just starting out cannot afford or get the financing to buy property.

In the future this will change. There will be no need for people to broker sales. All sales will be done directly between buyer and seller through home computers. There will be a central registry for all property available and for buyers to be registered as well. A government department will be responsible for all real estate transactions. Who will live where and when will be controlled so it does not get out of hand.

As things are now, older people still stay in their homes and take space in city cores where they can contribute nothing to the commercial area where they live. A place will be supplied for these people with everything they need for their comfort in a more peaceful setting. This will free the space they once occupied for those families that need the location to be near their work. It is foolish for so many to have to drive so many miles to work and back home every day.

There will also be no land set aside for cemeteries in the city proper. All burials of bodies or ashes will be controlled as to where and when they can be buried. It is ridiculous to have cemeteries on ocean-front locations within cities.

There will be more sites for garbage disposal outside of city limits. People will be regulated as to what they can dispose of and where they can dispose of it. Recycling will become a major industry.

More and more people will work at home rather than go to industrial plants and offices every day. New and faster computer systems will create a better method of working. There will be no trade barriers between nations or within nations. A new world order will make so many changes in people's lives that they will be astounded. There will be much more leisure time for everyone. Your workplace may well be your home. This does not mean all business can be done this way. There will still be those that need security in their operations, which is not possible with computers.

There will be less greed in the future, not because people will change, but because this will be forced upon them through necessity.

29. A NEW WORLD ORDER

The explosion of population in the world will soon make it obvious that the present system is not workable. There has to be a better sharing of world resources between the countries that have and those that have not. For too long, those in the best position to do so have ignored the plight of their fellow humans. It seems those who have the use of or can afford the most resources keep them for their own gain and wish not to share. To continue on this path will surely cause a chaotic world of discontent and mean severe conflict.

To bring about this sharing there must be a world order among all people. Each person in the world must have available to them what each needs. No longer will one country, because of its wealth and power, be able to dictate to other poorer countries what they can have. There must be a universal vote for those who lead, and each section of the world's population will have an equal number of representatives in this government. Of course, a great deal of education will need to take place before everyone can understand and make wise choices.

No longer will there be ethnic differences nor political groups trying to gain power. Safeguards must be put in place to prevent this. All food, medical supplies, and education will be shared equally. Gainful employment will be available for all people regardless of sex or race. Each individual must have the freedom to choose his or her method of sharing what they have to give by being employed.

Private enterprise that is nonpolluting and helpful to all must not have interference from government. Every person must be able to choose his or her own occupation as long as it is for the public good. There will be no unemployment because there will always be another job waiting when one disappears. Hardship will be at a minimum because of equitable rules and laws set up to prevent it. People will have a more satisfactory lifestyle because they will realize they have the same privileges as everyone else.

This does not mean that there will be no rewards for greater effort. It will be recognized, but will not be at the expense of their peers. The reward will be personal satisfaction about how he or she is thought about by his or her community. There will be no rewards that are physical, such as money or property. Greed, as I said before, will not be permitted.

30. JUSTICE

Born Many Times hastened to assure me that the last chapter was not what was going to happen in the very near future, but would be sometime in the future, brought about by necessity for the survival of the human race. I personally think some of it should happen now. He said the people were not ready for it yet. He then told me he would talk about law and order and the justice system we have in our time.

Laws are made by the community to make it easier for you to live together in harmony and security. They are intended to protect your property and your rights under the law. You have law officers appointed by your leaders to enforce these laws. You have courts where judges establish your innocence or guilt, or where you may be tried by a jury of people like yourself. If you are found guilty, the judge will punish you according to established rules. This could be by fines, imprisonment, or both, and sometimes by probation.

All people are supposed to be equal under the law. But this has proved not to be true. One's standing in the community and how well off one is financially have a bearing on the decisions of the courts of law. Appointments of judges and magistrates are sometimes made by the government, and this makes room for political bias. In some countries, the judges are elected and their decisions can still be politically motivated.

Nevertheless, the system works fairly well when the courts are open to the media who keep the public informed on what is going on there. This public scrutiny is the only way that real justice is likely to be gained. But the system is still faulty. There are too many repeat violators. There are still too many violators who do not get the punishment to fit the crimes committed. This is especially true when the crime is against women and minorities, though this is slowly changing.

Unfortunately, the prisons are overcrowded and overflowing with criminals. In some cases criminals are freed before their sentences are served in order to make room for other prisoners. The cost to punish these violators of the law is getting out of hand. The people who are not criminals are paying for those who are. Do you not wonder who is really being punished? It is time for humankind to look at alternatives to the system, especially when the present system is not working and does not rehabilitate those who commit crimes.

In the future, humankind will realize the system used for many centuries by the native peoples in North America is a better solution. The present concept that criminals are all bad has to be changed to a realization that they are sick and need curing. And you do not cure people by putting them in a cell in a jail. These people need to be re-educated. The present method keeps them in jail, and the contact with other criminals only makes them worse than when they were first imprisoned.

The problem must be attacked from the beginning. You must find out in each case why the person turned out the way he or she did. Two children from the same family and raised in the same way can be different. One can live a well-behaved life while the other can have criminal leanings. It is not an easy task to find out the cause for this, but there are some things which are obvious.

You have all seen a mother with young children in a supermarket take candy from a bin and give it to her children or take fruit from a counter and give it to her child without paying for it. This makes children believe that it is alright to take what you want any time you want it. They learn from observing the habits of their parents. They think it is okay to take things without paying. The truth is it is stealing, plain and simple, and people go to jail for this.

It is not only mothers and children who do this. We have all known adults and even seniors who do similar things. If they are caught and questioned they claim to be only testing the product to see if they like it. This is an outright lie, and they should know better. If the supermarket chose to lay a charge, this excuse would not hold up with any judge.

They say some people get this way because of the bad company they keep and so are led into crime. What nonsense! If a person were brought up with a moral feeling for his or her fellow man, he or she would not do wrong things no matter the provocation. Stealing to get money for drugs is a public responsibility. When a person, male or female, of any age, becomes so addicted as to commit crimes, the solution is to get the drugs out of circulation. But this has been proven to be impossible. Therefore, the only solution available is to treat and cure the addicted person.

Perhaps we should all look at ourselves in a mirror and ask what did we do or not do to contribute to making these things happen. The missing element in all the above is public condemnation. Because of their actions, were these people made to feel like outcasts from society or part of the community? If they had a sense of belonging to a community, it would be a dire punishment to be separated from it. It is up to all people no matter where they live to develop a sense of community and belonging.

But this doesn't happen; they are just fined or sent to prison. And in most cases when they have paid their fine or are released from prison, they are welcomed home with open arms into the community. They have paid their fines or have served their time, so they are free to continue on as before until caught again. Criminals often go on like this until some serious disaster strikes. Then the parents, who have brought them up to be as they are, blame society.

And in most cases they have a point. The community too easily forgets and forgives without proof that the criminals have learned a lesson. If a sick child needs medical attention that the parents cannot afford, the community often comes to their rescue by collecting the money needed from the people. After the child is cured, the same community takes pride in what it has done and the parents are grateful. A person who commits a crime is just as sick as that child, but we expect the law to punish him or her. Why does the law not punish the child for being sick?

This may seem extreme, but it is actually the same. They are both sick. The criminal is as sick as the alcoholic, drug user, or even the tobacco user. They need help and treatment as any sick person deserves. Therefore, putting a criminal into jail is not a good system, as has been proven. They need to be treated as the sick people they are.

The native peoples' system of justice places the emphasis on healing the one who has committed a crime against society, not on punishment. It begins with a Healing circle. Seated in the circle is the defendant's family, friends, and peers. Also present is the shaman, tribal chief and elders of the tribe. The group is seated with the defendant facing the family members.

An investigation is begun to find the reason for the defendant's behavior. Through questioning, his family members try to determine if they were responsible in any way for his behavior. This is a very stressful and emotional time for all concerned. But most important, it makes the defendant aware of the pain and suffering he has caused those who care for and love him.

Usually the Healing circle is sufficient to heal the defendant and make him aware that family, friends, and tribal community support him and want him healed. Very often the defendant responds and is ashamed of his actions. If this is not the case, more healing is done. Failing this, the next step is the one that usually cures those who have committed a crime. It is simply the separation of that person from the community for a long period of time with absolutely no contact with another human being. In isolation, he comes to realize how important community, family, and friends are, and regrets hurting those who loved and cared for him.

The person is isolated with no way of communicating with other people, and no telephone, radio, TV, or electricity. He is provided with food and warm accommodation, and that is all.

The native people use an isolated island for this purpose. This treatment does not take long to cure the person's illness. If he re-offends, the same procedure is followed, but for a longer period of time. He is informed that this will be his last chance to become a contributing member of the community. If he does re-offend after the third curing, he is then banished from the community forever. This means he is never allowed to contact or see his family, friends or any member of the community for the rest of his life. This stigma follows him wherever he goes, and in native societies no other group will accept him. This makes more sense than the treatment used now, which has proven to be useless.

31. GEOGRAPHICAL CHANGES

I was busy the next few weeks so I did not contact Born Many Times. This gave him time to attend to matters known only to himself. He told me that he had to do research to find out what I wanted to know, though he never told me where he did this research. He just brushed off the question with annoyance. I asked him about Earth changes in the future because there were so many futurists who gave different answers. He agreed to tell me what he could and continued.

Due to earthquakes, volcanoes and changes in ocean currents caused by the Earth's plates shifting, there will be changes to the Earth's weather patterns and landmasses. There will be a great loss of human life with these changes, so it may help some to know where they will be. First, I will tell you the worst that could happen.

The North American continent will be split into three continents. The eastern section will follow the St. Lawrence river through the Great Lakes, south along the Mississippi river to the Gulf of Mexico. It will stretch approximately from the Maritimes of Canada in the north down to the tip of Florida in the south, including the Caribbean islands. Its east side will follow the Atlantic ocean coastline while the west side will follow the St. Lawrence river through the Great Lakes and down the Mississippi to the Gulf of Mexico.

The middle continent will be from the north coast of Greenland to roughly the Panama canal. The western continent will be contoured from the Arctic to the tip of Baja. It will extend from Hudson Bay and Labrador with part of the Arctic including Greenland in the north to the Baja Sea in the south. On the eastern side it will follow the St. Lawrence river to the Great Lakes, then down the Mississippi to the Gulf of Mexico. On the western side it will flow down from Hudson's Bay to the Colorado river on to the Baja Sea.

The western section will go from Hudsons Bay and the Arctic along the Colorado to the Baja sea. On the western side it will be bounded by the Pacific ocean. It will extend from the Arctic in the north to the tip of Baja in the south.

The Pacific Ocean will be much smaller, but the water will be about the same level as it is now. The excess water will have gone between the three new continents, which will be separated on the average by about five hundred miles. These new continents will be called East America, Central America and West America.

What is presently South America will be divided into two continents along the Amazon basin to the Pacific ocean. These two new continents will be called North America and South America.

West America will move to the southwest. Central America along with Greenland will become one continent and will move almost due west. East America will remain in almost in the same location as it is now.

The new northern part of present-day South America will move slightly to the northeast, while the southern part will move southwest toward Australia. These new landmasses will be between five hundred and fifteen hundred miles apart.

This will be a gradual change and will not be completed until more than fifty thousand years have passed. It will cause a complete change in the ocean currents which will also affect temperatures. West and East America will become more tropical. Central America, and Greenland which will be part of it, will become temperate. Northern South America will be almost the same as it is now with the Tropic of Cancer just south of it. Southern South America will be much cooler in the north, with temperatures remaining almost the same as the present-day in the southern part.

Africa will slowly move to the south while Europe and Asia will be very little different as far as landmasses go, but will have a much different climate. The Orient will change a little. Japan, Korea, and other Pacific islands will join the mainland. China will have a large ocean where deserts now exist.

32. THE IMMEDIATE FUTURE

Again I tried to get Born Many Times to tell me what was in store for me and mine in the near future that we will be living in. He told me he did not want to influence what plans I had made for my own future and did not want to cause alarm among people. I asked him if it was cast in stone and he told me it was not. But the way things were at the present, the trend seems to be to this future. It can be changed if man acts now. He said he would go country by country as they exist in my time.

We will begin in your country, Canada, the north part of North America. Here the future could be excellent, but because of ethnic problems caused by your own government, you will face many difficulties. One problem is that you have two distinct nationalities, English and French, but no Canadian one. You are still tied to the apron strings of your mother countries in Europe.

For a country so large you have little population. You are really controlled by the powerful country to your south. This will change because its population will have their own problems that will be crucial to their survival. Really, the future belongs to your country. With more population and diverse ethnic backgrounds you can succeed in becoming an important world power in the coming centuries. But not until you learn to live together as a Canadian nation.

Unfortunately, there will probably be a vote on separation by the French-speaking population that will be confirmed. It may not be the next vote but it will happen. When it does, it will throw the country into chaos. The aboriginal part of the French province will not agree to separate along with a large number of French-speaking people. This will cause the rest of the Canadian public some concern for their safety. The Federal government will claim the vote to be unconstitutional, and this will turn the country to violence.

The separatists will become angry because their vote was not recognized and terrorist factions will emerge causing bloodshed on the streets. The rest of the country will turn on these people with violence of their own and this will cause more pain and bloodshed. France will threaten to intervene militarily and Britain and the United States will support Canada, so France will withdraw.

Eventually there will be a settlement, but not before the Federal government of Canada gives up most of its power to govern to the ten existing provinces. In effect, there will now be ten separate countries united in a group presumably for common good.

The United States, which is a prominent world power, is heading for a difficult future. The country is made up of people with different ethnic backgrounds which is one of the reasons why they have become so powerful. They have learned to live together pretty much for the common good of all. However, minorities will eventually dictate their policy toward other countries and this will be the biggest difficulty.

Citizens who have a mother country among enemies will influence their government where they live now to do things that will eventually do it harm. If they wish to exercise leadership, that leadership needs to be fair and impartial, which today it is not.

The justice that they preach is not the justice they practice. It is difficult to be all things to all people, and this is the most serious problem this country faces. If, with the best intentions, they help someone, they can hurt another, so it is a useless gesture.

It is very noble to help other people in other places, but help should stay at home where it belongs sometimes. When that help is given at a price to the person being helped, there will be future problems. There is always a price to pay. The foreign policy of the government will become so burdensome for some states that they will threaten to secede from the Union. Most important of these will be three of the richest states, California, Texas, and New York.

The Nafta agreement with Canada and Mexico will become a problem for all three countries. Mexico with its graft and lack of control over army and police will become too much of a burden for the States to bear. Their seeming refusal to stop drug and criminal activities will bring their own downfall.

Canada is less of a problem because it is controllable. Despite claims to the contrary, Canada is not as free as it thinks it is. Economically and politically, its survival depends on the United States. If the States were to refuse to accept any more trade with Canada, the Canadian economy would collapse along with its government. Canada can not look to Britain for help, for the British can barely care for themselves. Nor would any other country dare to offend the United States by helping.

In reality, the States has nothing to gain by doing this. Canada's relations with the States are excellent. Their agreements have historically mostly been of benefit to each other. Disagreements happen between friends, but this is no reason for violent behavior between them. They have usually had a common bond of friendship. In the future, there will be a closer bond between them.

Because of circumstances about to happen in the next century, Canada and the United States will become one country. Within the next fifty years this will happen and it will be a mutual decision. Because they are one people now, it should not be too difficult to accept. It will not be forced on them, but it will be for their own safety and security to do this.

Because of Canada having been split up into ten sovereign countries by the separation of French-speaking Quebec, many of these will entertain the thought of joining the States for their own security and protection. These sovereign countries could be a good addition to the United states financially and for raw materials.

The world will be thrown into chaos again with a conflict between old enemies, the United States and France. This will cause ill will between the United States and some of the European countries. Britain will not become involved, nor will some of the former Russian satellites.

There will be great disagreement and disappointment in the way the American government handles itself in the Israel-Palestine dispute, and this will mean the Arab world will also break off relations with the Americans within the next five years.

But enough of humanity and its problems, as there is more to worry about in the environment. There will be an increase in earthquakes, hurricanes, tornadoes, and flooding due to weather changes that will effect all areas of the northern continent.

The west coast of the United States will suffer the most from earthquakes, particularly the state of California.

The area from San Francisco south past the Mexican border and west to the Salton Sea will experience the worst of these earthquakes. There will be loss of life and many millions of dollars in property damages. The valley between Palm Springs and Desert Hot Springs will have a huge fissure appear between them. Most of the quakes will occur in poorly populated areas, but there will still be casualties.

In the ocean off Washington State and British Columbia, there will be a very large undersea quake that will do damage on shore and cause huge tidal waves. One of the largest quakes will occur in Alaska with many lives lost and a whole city destroyed.

Eastern U.S.A. and Canada will not escape altogether. There will be quakes where they have never occurred before. New York State will suffer a big one and, though not close to New York city, it will cause much damage there with some loss of life. The Provinces of Quebec and Ontario will also have some severe quakes, mostly in outlying districts.

Tornadoes will become common in the middle southern states and the whole eastern seaboard will suffer many hurricanes with loss of lives and great damage. Despite all this, the landmass will not be affected until the latter part of the new century. The central plains of North America will suffer from floods at the beginning of the twenty-first century and very dry conditions near the end.

All this will signal the beginning of the coming ice age, due to start by the end of the fifth century in the future. This will be a long, slow process and not something that will be noticeable at the start. The Earth's population will have plenty of time to relocate to safer places.

33. THE ABORIGINAL PEOPLE

I asked Born Many Times to pause and give some thought to native peoples of northern continent comprising the United States and Canada could hope for in the future. He was more than delighted to talk about them because he had spent so many lifetimes among them. He told me that of all the people he had ever met they were his favorites.

From their beginning in time, these people have suffered, first with the elements and then with other of their species, mankind. In ancient times they had to face terrible obstacles to survive. Those that came over the land bridge from the Orient left a country where winter never ceased and where they were hunted down like animals. When they crossed the land bridge to escape, they still faced the bitter weather.

Some continued east and are the Intuit of today. Others went south along the coast and are now the western coastal Indians of North America. The ones that went east lived as they did before. Those that went south had a better life. With plenty of fish and animals to eat and a warmer climate, they prospered. That is, until the white man arrived.

The natives to the south came from other countries and islands from the Pacific, mostly from Atlantis, which had disappeared beneath the Atlantic ocean. They prospered and lived in almost all of North and South America. When they arrived, they spread out over nearly all of this great land. They had endured a very dangerous trip here and had to get used to a strange land. There were animals, serpents, and diseases that were strange to them. They also had an unsettled landmass with numerous earthquakes, hurricanes, flooding and weather changes.

With the help of Atlanteans some developed great civilizations and built huge cities with remarkable architecture. They had city states that are the envy of people even today. But over time came the human element of greed and desire for possessions. Some of their leaders wanted more and this caused continual warfare among them, as it has for the white man. Greed and warfare are the only bad things that the white man didn't bring into this part of the world. They already existed.

It is ridiculous to say that these people, here only a short time, gained or had the knowledge to build such huge pyramids, temples and observatories without help from visitors from outer space. Nor could they have done so much in agriculture and developed plants that had not existed before without this help. Even today with all your science and knowledge you cannot duplicate this.

But there is one thing that the North American natives had that the white man will never have or take away from them, and this is their religion—their ability to live with nature and each other as one, which caused their love of the Great Spirit and their obedience to this Spirit. To them, this Great Spirit is in every thing, no matter what, as long as it is alive. Love and life to them was the Great Spirit, and all life helped each other. The Great Spirit was never considered to be a man but was all things, because He was within all things.

Wherever they looked they could see the Great Spirit, whether it was in a small flower or a beautiful sunset. They could see the Great Spirit in a baby's face, a tree, a meadow, a reptile, any animal or bird, in fact, everything. One cannot imagine the exhilaration they felt when they realized that they were part of all this. Every one of us should. If you want to see a miracle, then open your eyes and look.

Never mind the computer that does so many things, the car that one can travel in in such comfort or the airplane that seems to defy gravity and makes you feel like a bird. All man does or creates pales in comparison with what the Great Spirit has created. In fact, look at yourself. The Great Spirit has given you an amazing body and mind and the power to create another human being.

Man can create many things, but by himself he cannot create life. He can prolong it with medicine and surgery, but he cannot create it. When all is said and done, all life must cease when the right time comes. No matter the cause, it will still happen to all some day. Life is a miracle happening, and so is death.

These are the things that the native people built their beliefs and lives upon. The community was the very lifeline to them all. When the white man came to these shores where the natives had lived for untold centuries, he came with ideas that were strange and not easily understood. But the white man in his ignorance and through the blessings of the church soon taught these savages the error of their ways.

Not being content to take the native's lands and to change their lifestyles, customs and religion, the white man put them into what he called reservations. In later times when white men fought each other they called such reservations concentration camps. How can they be called concentration camps for white men and for the natives reservations? Is there a difference? Perhaps because they were ashamed of what they were doing to the native peoples they tried to call them something more humane? If so, this shame should exist even today. They still call these concentration camps reservations.

The United Nations, which is supposed to help and protect subjugated and abused people, is just a big farce. Never have they done anything for the native peoples and they probably never will. How does the world react when they hear about how the native children were forcibly taken from their families to live in a school far from their homes, to be taught the white man's ways and punished if they ever mentioned anything native? Lately the sexual abuse of these children has come to light, and the law is doing something about it. But the schools were run by the Christian churches who denied for years that this was happening.

Well, the world of the white people has something else to be ashamed about. Lately in your time there have been native people who have voiced their concerns about their treatment. This will never change things as long as they speak in different voices. They must become united with one voice and then they will get results. Too long they have suffered separately and been divided. Now they must have one voice to be heard. If there is one thing I can see in the future, this is the most pronounced possibility.

34. OTHER POLITICAL CHANGES

Because Born Many Times as well as I were sympathetic with the Native Americans, it was a painful experience to talk about them. It makes me ashamed of being a white human being. It is inconceivable that one race of humans could and can still treat another race of humans in this way. But there were other things that I was waiting to hear from him, and he said he would confide in me what mankind would be facing in the near future.

I will deal first with the changes in Russia that will affect other countries. Early in the new century, their leader, Boris Yeltsin, will be replaced with the old communist regime. Their new leader will be the man Yeltsin fired from his position during the past year. He will become the supreme leader as Stalin was and will be just as tough.

Because Russia has suffered bad economic times the people will think anything will be better. The new government will become just as much a threat to democratic governments as it was before. Because it still has a large storage of strategic nuclear weapons, it will not be an easy government to get along with. It will find it has a lot to do to regain its lost prestige and will take risks to get it back.

Because China is a communist country, there will be an understanding between the two old enemies for their common good. Before 2010, they will forge an alliance and become a joint threat to world peace.

China will annex Taiwan despite resistance from the United States. There will be a general shifting of support throughout the Asian community. The Philippines will be more open to Asian overtures and will join them politically. Hong Kong will be treated like the rest of China despite promises that it will be otherwise.

There will be a shifting of economic and political loyalties within the Asian governments. They will combine to become the leading economic world force in this century, outperforming the United States and its allies. Australia will be the only country in this area that will maintain its independence.

Sometime in the 2020's, all of Canada will have become another state of the United States, joining Mexico, which will also become part of the States. Cuba, along with all the Caribbean islands, will join the United States. This will not happen without the approval of the people in these countries. It will be because it is a matter of security and safety.

The United States will by force take the Panama Canal and those countries next to it for the security of all the countries in the area. All other countries in South America will become one country for their own protection and security. They will remain friendly to those in the north. This will not happen without bloodshed. The biggest holdouts will be Columbia and Peru, which are now under the control of foreign powers.

Before 2005, The United States will invade Columbia and destroy the drug cartels that exist there. After they have done this, they will not be interested in occupying this country. Castro of Cuba will either be assassinated or die naturally within the next ten years, and the country will become a protectorate of the United States as will all the Caribbean islands.

There will be no global conflicts for the first five hundred years of the century, but after that a world order will have to be established under the guidance of advice from other worlds. There will be threats and even some battles, and peace will be shaky but it will come. The European community will become more like one country, along with those countries that were part of the old Soviet empire.

The British Commonwealth of nations will cease to exist. The United Nations will disappear and will be replaced by a world body that is more equitable to all countries. There will be no vetoes for any country. No one will have the power to demand obedience of its decisions without full discussion and agreement of all members.

35. THOSE OUT OF THIS WORLD

The last chapter was not easy for me to write or understand fully because such changes were so great. But when I thought about the changes during the last thousand years, my perspective improved. I now realize that all things are possible and this made me feel better about the future. I realized that the haves will not always be the haves, and the have nots will not always be the have nots. We must, as dwellers on this planet, be able to share what it has to offer equally. No longer will there be people who can take the bigger share at the expense of others.

Born Many Times was ecstatic about what I had grasped and said from now on I could not take a bite of an apple as long as there were people who did not have an apple to bite. I now mentioned that in a previous talk he had alluded to other worlds, and asked what he meant. He said he thought I was ready to accept what he was about to tell me, but had reservations about my readers. I told him I wanted to know what he had to say and the readers could come to their own conclusions. They could accept it or not.

There have been so many reports about extraterrestrial beings visiting Earth from somewhere in outer space. These reports are quoted in historical documents and even in the Holy Bible. But still humankind does not accept that they exist. There are those who will not believe the world is round, but that it is square if that is what they were taught. Then there are those who believe in the Biblical Creation, though it has been proved beyond a doubt that the world predates what the creationists claim.

This is not just theory, but hard physical evidence. It is foolish to compare what mankind has written with the hard science of discovery. How could evidence of man living on Earth be found going back one hundred thousand years when creationists say it was all created six thousand years ago? So even with hard evidence there are still those who do not believe that there is life in other parts of our universe.

One of the problems that brings about this disbelief is the claim of some that they have been taken captive aboard a spacecraft and have had experiments done on them. Some try to deceive the public by making phony movies about the spacecraft. What benefit do they derive from this? Surely they will gain nothing but ridicule when found out.

But there is solid evidence that is hard to explain away. Some of the people taken aboard a spacecraft have scars and implants to show of their experience. It is well known that governments suppress documented information about landings and alien contacts. There are landing sites that clearly show tripod landing feet of the craft. There are often high amounts of radioactivity there. Scientists still have not given satisfactory answers about crop circles. Sure a few of them are man-made, but hundreds all over the world could not have been.

Believe it or not, there have been extraterrestrials visiting your Earth in the past and right up to the present day. So far, there has been no public scrutiny of any physical evidence to confirm their existence. This is because the governing bodies where this evidence has been confiscated and kept have covered it up and kept it secret. They do this to protect certain powerful interests, the most important being the religious businesses, no matter their denominations. Whether Christian, Muslim, Buddhist, or Islamic, they would shortly become obsolete if this truth were known.

During the first century of the new millennium, all present-day religions will disappear due to the visits by people from other worlds in our Universe. This means that the whole Universal system will become available to every Earth being, and they will learn that things are not as they have been taught. The most important thing they will learn is that humankind is not the most important life form that exists.

Other life forms in the Universe will prove to be more advanced in intelligence than they are. This should not be too hard to comprehend, because even in your world there are more natural life forms with more intelligence than humankind, such as microbes and bacteria.

In the new millennium, coming soon, but probably not in the lifetime of those living now, there will be indisputable proof of extraterrestrial's existence and earthlings will have to accept the fact. All the man-made falsehoods we have come to accept as the truth will go. This will be a shock that some will not be able to accept, and mass suicides will become more common than they are now. But fortunately, those who do believe and accept the truth will be happier and more content than before.

You will be shown how a new world order will be of benefit to you if you are willing to replace the system you presently have. All the world's resources will be made available to all the people in the world if they choose to have them. This does not mean luxury items but the necessities of life. There is no need for a man at the North Pole to have an automobile. But then, there will be no automobiles anyway.

Many other things that you have come to accept will not be needed in the future. One of these is trade unions because they will not be necessary. Workers will not need a union to negotiate with themselves, nor will they strike against themselves because in the future, with the new system, they will be working for themselves. They will be their own employers.

There will be no commerce as it exists today, nor will there be money used as exchange. Everyone will live on credit, which will be obtained by one's work for the common good of all. The use of personal computers will be commonplace, not for fun and games, but of necessity. Most employees will work from their homes, making huge offices and buildings unnecessary.

Most manufacturing and assembly plants will run on computers and robots. This will make much of the manpower redundant. There will be no need for environmental controls because everything now being wasted will be used and reused. There will be no need for landfill sites, as all garbage will be recycled into useful and needed things. Air pollution will be a thing of the past as air cleaners will keep chemicals and solid matter out of the air.

There will be no more pollutants in water. Water will be recognized as a national resource and greater care will be made to keep it pure and clean. All this will not become reality because of laws and rules imposed on society. The cause will be a great catastrophe that will make the Earth almost uninhabitable because of pollution and neglect. Much of the Earth's population will die because of this, forcing humanity to act for its own survival.

There will be changes in the new millennium, but they will take place over time. There will be earth-shattering volcanoes, earthquakes, and climatic changes as the new century begins. These changes will occur over a period of time and mankind will make plans to adapt out of necessity and for their own survival. But the environmental changes that have come about in the last fifty years will accelerate in the future. Many of these changes will be by accretion.

36. A QUESTIONABLE PERIOD

My mind was now a seething cauldron of information; some of it I understood, most of it I did not. I knew mankind had a lot to do to if it were to survive in the future much as it had since the beginning of time. The idea of foreign visitors to our planet from other galaxies was acceptable to me as I had become accustomed to this way of thinking from the strange things being reported almost daily. I had seen strange objects move through the skies. But whether these visitors were friendly or otherwise was still a matter of uncertainty to me.

If they were going to act towards us as we have acted towards our fellow humans in the past, I was concerned. We are all aware that those with a higher civilization have usually enslaved and treated like animals those with lower technology or less power. Look what happened in Africa, India, and North and South America. Then again, I knew it was only because of the ignorance of those in power that such suffering was inflicted.

If these beings are as intelligent as they are reported to be, surely they will not show such ignorance. Born Many Times assured me they were coming here to help us, not to rule us. What they can teach us will be for our survival and that of the universe. The most important thing they will be able to confirm is that there is a god and that He loves us.

We will learn that we should not spend our lifetime fearing death or god, but realize that it is just a part of living and we shall go right on living after we die here.

I asked Born Many Times if he would tell me about alien visitors to our planet and he agreed to do so.

I have often mentioned that mankind's history on this Earth is much, much older than your scientists care to admit or investigate. They have a collective mind-set and allegiance to theories that they will never admit are wrong, nor will they admit that anything else is possible other than what they collectively believe. There has been ever so much evidence that they have refused to investigate because this might interfere with their beliefs.

This, of course, will be their own undoing. In time their science will be subjected to scorn because they have been so closed-minded. How can one believe they are true scientists if they do not investigate every shred of evidence that is put before them? This they will not do, because they would rather accept the status quo. Those that have had the courage to do some real investigation (and there have been many) are held up to ridicule by their peers.

I must admit that these academics have to rely on governments and other vested interests to finance their investigations and so are controlled by special interest groups. For the past two thousand years, the churches have used their influence to stop any investigation into history that does not conform to their point of view. It is a wonder that the Darwinian theory of evolution ever became accepted in the face of the opposition by the churches. They would prefer that people accept the creationism theory instead, which is in accord with their beliefs.

But the more people have become educated and gained the ability to think for themselves, the more they have become independent in their thinking. Despite what the established religions and other special interest groups want, people are demanding that they be given truthful answers to the origins of their species, and they will not be denied. In the past, many people who argued against the dogma of the churches were punished and even put to death. I have talked to some of these people from the past in their present state of consciousness. They show no anger because they have found the real truth, which you all will some day.

Many times the Bible mentions visitors from outer space and the vehicles they used. Every group of people that has lived on this Earth has historical stories about visitors from the heavens. The aboriginal natives everywhere have legends handed down from times past about heavenly visitors. Today thousands of people have had experiences to do with space ships or visitations. Still the majority of people refuses to believe them. But they will all become convinced soon.

Early in the next hundred years there will be conclusive proof presented that will make it impossible not to believe. Beings will arrive here and make contact with your government figures, who will have no choice but to accept them. They will be friendly and helpful and will make a positive contribution to your survival in the universe.

But, as usual, there will be a high cost to pay. All your preconceived ideas regarding life and religion will change dramatically. Everything that has been learned and practiced for centuries by earthlings will change.

Those who cannot or will not accept these changes will be set aside. They will not be harmed in any way, but will be given time to accept the new way things are.

Moral obligations and rules of behavior within human society will become paramount. People will accept these new ways because they will see the immediate benefit of doing so. No longer will there be someone or something outside of your own being influencing your decisions. Your own inherent goodness will prevail without outside pressure. There will be no more prisons or punishment needed. Anyone doing illegal acts—which will be rare—will be given a chance to gain a cure for their trespasses through a healing educational treatment. Those who cannot accept this will be taken to a place where they will have no contact with others of their kind until they are cured.

Greed and jealousy will disappear from your perception of things. There will be no need for either of these emotions to exist. Everyone will share in the world's resources, and harmony and trust will be everyday feelings within human consciousness.

Your knowledge of the Universe will expand, and exploration of other planets and universe will become commonplace for those qualified to do so.

Even if the majority of you do not have the opportunity to visit faraway places, you will have information through education about them. Even today in your world there are places you have not visited and never will. Earthlings will have so much to learn, it will take centuries before they can begin to grasp the immensity of it all.

This will not be the first time these visitors have come among us. They have made many visits to our planet in the past. They developed numerous civilizations on our planet in ancient times. Perhaps earthlings should look at the myths and old stories told by aboriginal people to learn about these. The first people contacted by these visitors were the Atlanteans and the people of Mu. When their homelands disappeared, they spread throughout the world, leaving their marks and knowledge with others.

Some of these marks are in the Mediterranean area and in South America. This is how these formerly primitive people learned to build such enormous cities of stone, and how to decorate these stones with beautiful carvings. They also learned ways to increase the quantity and quality of their crops. They learned to diversify and rotate their crops and were given seed for crops they never had before. Even today, you are still the beneficiary of this knowledge and of these crops. For example, archaeologists have never been able to trace the origin of maize or corn. Native people say it was given them by visitors from the sky.

Despite their voiced wishes to the contrary, these visitors began to be worshipped as gods. We all know the Greeks had numerous gods they worshiped, as did the Romans, Druids and Celts. It was so with the Maya, Inca, Toltecs, Olmecs, and Aztecs. All these different people had visitors from space and many others we do not have recorded history of.

Why do you think the people of South America, England, and Europe made huge petra forms or drawings that could only be seen and recognized from the air when these people did not have any aircraft available to see them? There are even petra forms just north of Blyth, California, and in other areas of North America whose construction can't be explained away as just a pastime for natives.

The time, work and planning of such huge drawings must have been done for more than just fun and games. They were a message to people who could see them from above the Earth in some kind of craft. The only people who could see them in those times were people from outer space who had spacecraft.

Why were models of aircraft made and pictures drawn of them back when they did not exist? Why did the people who had wheels for children's toys not make them larger and use them for practical purposes? They had beasts of burden they could have used to pull them, but they did not. They even had roads that could be used for such vehicles, but they were not put to this use.

The truth is they did not need them. The visitors had machines that did not require wheels because they flew above the ground. There is one petroglyph in Maya country that plainly shows a Mayan man using such a vehicle. It has controls for the man's hands and feet and flame jetting out behind. This shows a man driving a jet sled of some kind.

It is well known that roads connected all the great cities of the Mayan culture which were later destroyed by the Spanish to keep the Mayan separated. There is evidence of these roads that can still be seen today. They were made of stones carefully placed to make a flat surface through the jungle. There are roads still being used today that once connected areas of the Inca empire. There were even rest areas for the travelers along these roads.

In closing, I can only say that I have personally seen and talked with these visitors from other planets and can assure you they only want to inform and help you. If you think they are a threat to you, how do you think they feel about you? If you think about it realistically would you want to bother with you?

37. LET'S TAKE A LOOK

What Born Many Times said rather stuck in my craw. I did not think we were so bad. After all, we have social programs to help those that need help. Most people contribute to charities from the goodness of their hearts. We have formed the United Nations to try to prevent wars from starting and to promote peaceful negotiations in disputes. This group of nations also has tried to help the poorer ones to improve their lot. The richer countries have contributed to the well being of the poorer nations.

They have even sent peacekeepers to problem areas at their own expense. They have tried to set and make available minimum educational standards for all people. Medical treatment and supplies are given where there is need. People in "have" countries try to help those that "have not." There are Foster Parent plans to give people a chance to adopt children that need help, thus giving it a personal appeal. Food and clothing are continually being collected for needy families.

So what did he mean by saying, "Would you realistically want you to visit you?" I think we do pretty damn well. We tithe at churches, we pay our taxes to support social programs, we donate money, clothes, and food to charities. We pay a fixed amount of money every month to adopt a foster child in some foreign country that we will probably never see. We allow immigrants to come to our countries to get a better life for themselves and a better future. What else can we possibly do? Born Many Times was quick to answer.

In my lifetimes I have seen unsavory things and people and circumstances, but I never get angry at the ignorance of man for I am used to it. But I am surprised at you, because I thought that you, of all people, would know better. And then again I know you do, because you are only speaking with the tongue of what most men think today. You are merely giving the side of the argument that people would make in your time.

We both know that all the problems you have mentioned, where you are giving to solve them, were caused by people in the first place. Let us take each one separately. They were not caused by you or any individual personally, but all of you collectively. Man is aware of the effects of what he does, but does nothing to eliminate the cause.

Richer nations use the poverty of poorer nations to their own ends. They use the cheaper labor of these nations, whether producing bananas or automobiles, for their own benefit. They do not seem to care if the people make a suitable living wage as long as they satisfy their own interests, which is to produce products that can make larger profits than if produced in their own countries, where labor is more expensive.

The poorer nations have to accept this because a meager wage is better than no wage at all. So the people suffer. This means they cannot afford to support an educational system for their children. They cannot afford better houses for shelter or more and better food for their families. Their health suffers. So they have to ask richer nations to help them cope.

Usually poorer nations are governed by corrupt officials and politicians who are in the hands of the richer nations. So they are in a no-win situation. To say that most of you are not aware of this is false, but still you do nothing about it.

Most people who have a high standard of living do not concern themselves with people who do not. They feel that the others should take care of themselves.

So when the poor nations do rebel out of desperation, they are again criticized by those who have plenty. They send in their armies disguised as peace missions to bring what they call law and order to these less fortunate people. They did not worry before when they were so subjugated, and had no law or power on their side. If the rebels do win and form a government they feel will help them to a better life, they find that the richer nations will no longer deal with them and so have worse poverty than they had before.

Even in the richer nations you have problems with unemployment, and people have to seek welfare for various reasons. In some cases the people are too old to work and must be supported. Sometimes people do not have the skills to find meaningful employment. There are dozens of reasons why people must seek welfare. But there is not one that cannot be corrected. If there is a will, there is always a way.

Mankind is, for some reason, a war-making animal. There has never been a time in recorded history when man has not made war on others of his kind. He does this to gain superiority over the other. Even in a harmless sport activity this still is the goal of the contest. To gain superiority over another. This also translates into everyday business practice. There is never a time when people are not trying to be better off than their neighbors.

Even your entertainment business is geared to show one person getting the better of another. You have to be the better lawyer, doctor, lover, be more handsome, smarter, or richer than others. Television and movies portray violent and illegal means to get what is desired. If you want money, you just find a rich man and kill him and take his money or, if you are a woman, seduce, and marry him. If you want sex you find a suitable woman and rape her. Such is entertainment. If you complain about this violence in the media you are accused of interfering with others' rights to watch what they want.

If you were a person from another galaxy, would you walk into a mess like this? Do not think for a moment that they do not know what goes on here on your planet. You have been observed for countless centuries. But the sky people know that not all people are bad or uncaring. That is why they never give up on you. They know that what I have described will not continue very much longer.

Forces that you are completely unaware of are at work doing things every minute of every day that will correct these things. These forces have nothing to do with religion of any kind. You feel these forces in earthquakes that are becoming more numerous, flooding being suffered more often, climatic change, and cosmic developments mankind has not yet seen. During the next five hundred years, there will be changes in the Earth you can not even imagine possible.

But this is not the first time that the Earth has suffered through many changes. As I have told you, it has happened many times, changing and sometimes destroying civilizations. Sometimes humankind has been able to keep its society intact, but usually it has returned to a more primitive state. It is a matter of how much change and damage has been done and the amount of the loss of life that has come about.

If there is a great loss of leaders, technical and scientific personnel, it takes longer for the people to regain what has been lost. It is hard to rebuild without proper direction. To have shelter and food is always the first priority. It is surprising how soon the loss, pain, and destruction is forgotten in the effort to survive in new surroundings. It is not just humans who have to make adjustments; the animal population has just as many adjustments to make.

If it happens here, the visitors will be there as they have been in the past to help rebuild your lost civilization. It will probably not be the same as before but will be patterned after their own. This is what happened in both Egyptian and Mayan civilizations when they were taken from being primitive to highly civilized people in a very short period. This has been going on for hundreds of thousand years. And do not think that the visitors have not experienced the same problems on their own planets.

It seems to be a natural thing for humankind to build advanced civilizations only to have them destroyed and have to rebuild them time and time again. In the past, these visitors came and helped to rebuild civilizations after they were destroyed. This time, they will arrive here to help prevent the cause of the damage, so it does not need to come about. Your own civilization has been progressing for centuries. In the past century it has progressed at an alarming rate.

Your science has worked hard to conquer nature and change it to your own benefit. Scientists have not even considered what effect they are having on other life forms and in some cases even their own. They feel they have conquered nature, but this is ridiculous. The laws of nature were put into place by god, and no man can change them. Oh, they may think they have done so successfully, but they deceive themselves.

Humankind is just now becoming aware that the natural way or the way nature was programmed by a Higher Source is the best way. Most of your food products that science has claimed to have improved upon were developed by nature over millions of years through trial and error to make them the best possible for you.

People today are turning to organic food for good reason. It is more nutritious and has no chemical additives. Most illnesses today can be traced to the chemicals ingested with food. All fruits and vegetables can be organically grown without such fertilizers and they taste better and are healthier. Meat and poultry products have suffered the same fate. Chemicals injected into the animals and poultry to keep them alive and growing faster remain in the meat to contaminate you.

Science has not only contaminated the food you eat, but also the air you breathe. You are all aware of the pollution that has fouled your air. Cutting trees is lowering the oxygen supply in the air, and this is something you cannot live without. Tree cutting has caused soil erosion that has damaged the streams and rivers, and this has affected the fish stocks that need these streams and rivers for survival. When the trees are made into pulp for paper, the chemicals used are then dumped into the water, causing even more pollution.

There is a lot of air pollution caused by these paper mills, but this is only one industry that causes pollution. Every manufacturing process causes some chemical fallout, either during the manufacturing or through the product that is used afterwards.

So it appears that everything wrong with your world is caused by you and no one else. If there is a change to be made it will have to be made by you. No one else is going to make the decision to change things. No amount of praying to a Supreme Being can reverse it. No visitor from another part of the Universe will bring it about. No one but you and the will to do it.

As my name suggests, I have had many lifetimes here on your Earth and I have seen many great civilizations come and go. But yours is different. The world has become a smaller place with transport and communication. People are closer together and ethnic backgrounds, though important to each individual, need to be forgotten for the common good of all people. If you understand that you are all citizens of the world and that world is all you have, you will realize you must take good care of it.

In the past, there were only petty little pockets of control which we refer to as empires. When these disappeared for one reason or another, they only disturbed the people in that little pocket, but today there is no longer room for little pockets of empires. Today, what you do, individually or collectively, influences what happens in your whole world today. With your modern methods of communication, everyone can learn what every one else is doing.

38. CONVERSATIONS WITH AN ALIEN

During the five weeks after my last conversation with Born Many Times, I had a feeling that I had missed something that I should have picked up on. Suddenly, I realized that the one thing that was left unexplained to my satisfaction was Born Many Times's reference to alien visitors to our planet from other worlds in the Universe. There was more information to be had regarding these extraterrestrial visitors, and I knew Born Many Times had this information.

After a difficult time trying to contact him, he appeared on the scene again. He seemed disturbed and wanted to know what information I wanted now. I explained that I felt I needed to know more about the alien visitations to our planet. Could he help me? He was reluctant at first, then suddenly agreed to do what he could, not to just satisfy my knowledge, but to help others understand what they were faced with in the future. He began:

Humans of this world have great misconceptions about other worlds. They are so arrogant about their own evolution that they think themselves to be superior to other forms of life that inhabit the Universe. Why must all intelligent life be in the same form you are? Must they look like you? The life forms in other galaxies realize that since you are primitive people, you will not accept other life forms more intelligent than yours if they do not appear as you do.

In a lifetime past, I met a person who was an alien living amongst you. This man who came to my attention was using mental telepathy to converse with someone I was not aware of.

He noticed me looking at him strangely and approached me. He never spoke a word but conversed with me by thought transference. He asked me where I was from, and when I told him, he was surprised that I was able to use mental telepathy as well as he could.

I told him I was not of this world but was from a spirit plane of consciousness and could go from one plane to another at will. I then noticed something strange about him that would not be apparent to other living mankind. He had no soul. He was a humanoid, manufactured in the likeness of man. He knew instantly what I was thinking and confirmed what I had guessed.

He was showing great concern, and I hastened to assure him his secret was safe with me. I noticed, as he did, that we were getting curious glances from people passing by. They could not understand why two grown men would stand on the sidewalk, looking at one another without speaking. We both smiled at this and decided to find a more private place to continue our mental conversation.

We took a taxi to a waterfront park nearby and sat on a bench facing a small lake. It was a serene, quiet place and very private. People were walking along a path by the lake, but they paid no attention to us. He looked to be about forty-three or so. He laughed and told me he was more than two hundred of your years old. I was very surprised at this, and he said he had permission to tell me what was puzzling me.

He said that the world where he was made is very different from yours. To begin with, there are no relationships such as you have. The male and female of their species are not like you are. There is no obvious way to tell the sex of these beings as there is no discernable way to see any difference between them. He did not tell me what their appearances are. Instead he kept this information and that of other humanoids to himself.

They had the means to make life forms such as he with complete accuracy, and after many centuries they perfected the science of making humanoids with great reliability.

An Extraterrestrial Humanoid

Knowing they themselves would never venture from their planet, they decided to make these humanoids to do it for them. The first ones they made did not resemble beings from this world at all. There have been many reports in your world of these first robots being sighted and described.

They were short with a small frame. They had large heads with big protruding eyes. People here call them grays. They were robots or clones of each other. They were made to be able to fit into small flying vehicles to gather specimens from other galaxies. They had a very limited intelligence and were only able to perform the tasks assigned to them.

These grays were the first to come to your world, and many reports have been made of them experimenting on your people. They were not really doing experiments, but were gathering certain minute body parts needed in their own galaxies. These small parts were needed to make humanoids such as himself. They used cells as well as other similar materials to manufacture the humanoids. Some of these parts were gathered from other worlds besides your own, and many parts are not from beings like you. They were able to make and clone both male and female humanoids from these parts. He explained:

"When we were finally made to their satisfaction, we were then trained in their respective tasks. We were sent by a much larger spacecraft to different worlds such as your own to gather information related to the world we were visiting. I was sent to this world. Here, I gather information that is held in a memory bank in your world and transferred to my own when needed.

"It is not necessary for us to have large transmission stations to keep in touch with each other, because we use telepathy to communicate. We can do this safely because the people of your world are not " telepathic." In other words, they are not able to communicate in the manner which you and I are doing right now. We have not spoken with each other by any other means.

You are the first human I have found on this world that can do this. My owners are concerned about this. But you have said you are not of this world either.

"I must observe and reason about you for our safety. That is why I have been frank with you, because I have no choice. You, too, can read my mind. But I am having trouble exploring yours and this is causing much alarm among my owners. They wonder if you are one of those—by this I mean one of the humanoids who have developed some trouble and cannot be controlled by my owners. These are usually destroyed immediately, but my owners cannot do this to you because you have a soul, which I do not.

"It appears you are a mystery to them and they want me to continue communicating with you until the problem is solved. Your mind is sometimes closed to me and I cannot read you. I know you wish me no harm and are just as curious about me as I am about you. You must realize that people here cannot destroy me because I am replaced immediately. I am not human, but the results of years of experiments in the place where I was made.

"It bothers you that I do not have a soul as you have. Let me explain this. First, because I do not have a soul does not mean that I do not have a consciousness and am not spiritual in all my actions. I am not here to hurt anyone nor to do any harm. I am made to help the people of this planet. I have been instilled with the thoughts of my maker, who is of the highest spiritual fabric.

"Your scientists have put their efforts into building such a being as I am, but they have used materials that will never meet the standards that my maker has used. They have recently learned to clone animals and have shown interest in cloning their own likeness. This is repulsive to the majority of your people on religious or spiritual grounds. This is also true where I was made. I am not a copy of my makers. I am a copy of you, but not a clone of any one individual here.

"If it were possible for you to go to a new planet and be able to observe the inhabitants, would you not want to appear as they are? Suppose they did not look like yourself. What if they were still in a very primitive stage of development? What if the prime intelligence that did exist was you? That you had authority over all living things on your planet. That you killed and ate other living beings on your planet. That you made war on each other, let others of your kind starve to death, let others more powerful than some dominate them. Tell me, do you have a soul?

"No, I do not have a soul, but I do none of the things that you, who has one, do. As is usual, the people of your planet judge things from their own environment and cultures. But this is not the way things are judged by a stranger coming to your planet. To us you are like wild animals in your actions. If we wanted to we could, with hardly any effort, destroy you and your world.

"But we are truly civilized and would never do such a thing. It is better to work to make you good citizens of the Universal community than to destroy you. By destroying you, it would make us as bad as you appear to us to be.

"We, the humanoids, are made up of minute parts of many different humans from different planets of the Universe. We were made to look like you so we can work here unobserved. We take many different forms to work on other planets for the same purpose. You, too, are really made from parts of planets that carried the building blocks of life to your Earth over millions of years. You are not just made from this Earth; you are truly made from parts of the whole Universe.

"Your life forms have developed over many centuries, influenced by the sun, and have become what they are. Not all life forms are the same. Not all life forms can survive the atmospheric and chemical conditions here that make you what you are. In other planets different-appearing life forms have developed, using the conditions there to become what they are. Not all life forms are the same. Not all life forms can survive in the other conditions such as different atmospheric gases and pressures and the lack of sunlight for the proper temperature. Living conditions between planets differ immensely.

"So, when the scientists on my home planet took matter from many planets and gave it life, it was a tremendous breakthrough. This gave them the opportunity to observe other life forms in other places. I am only one of the types of life forms they created; there are many different kinds used on other planets. In the early years of our experiments, many life forms were developed that proved to be useless. When they sent them to the planets to be explored, their appearance sometimes caused panic.

"Our early humanoids, which are still in use, are the ones that are known by all people in other planets. It became useless to avoid detection because of their appearance and the many times they were used. These are the small or short ones with the big eyes and small pointed features. They have long thin legs and arms and thin fingers. These were the first ones made by our scientists. They needed the humanoids to be small because of the limited space on their early spacecraft. Humanoids my size were too big to be transported in the crafts they had at that time.

"These grays, as they are known here, are called pods on our planet. They are placed on spacecraft after being programmed as to what they are to do. They are not activated until they have landed on your planet. Upon landing, they go about their assigned tasks. They do not communicate with each other since they know exactly what they're to do. This is usually gathering samples of tissue of living life forms on your planet. No one, and I stress this point, has ever been kidnaped by our people and taken on board a spacecraft. These craft are far too small for a person from Earth to enter.

"No human from your planet has ever been sexually molested or impregnated by our people. They may have taken eggs from the females and sperm from the males, and that is all. There has never been a conversation between a pod and an earthly human, because the pods simply cannot talk. They are only capable of making a small squeaking noise to give an alarm to each other when necessary. They have never killed a human to get samples, but they have killed other animals because large samples were necessary. We have learned of the pain this has caused people when a beloved pet has been killed, and now they are careful to take only wild animals for this purpose. But very few samples are required now.

"I must also stress that the people from our planet have never been on a spacecraft, simply because they would not survive such a voyage. Because of the difference in air and atmosphere, they would not be able to stay alive here in any case. Your scientists must change their plans to send humans into space to far-off planets. They will never find the means to get them there and back again. They would perish on the trip. What you have accomplished up to now is about the limit of your explorations of space.

"You have been able to make mechanical means to gather evidence from the closest planets to yours, and now you must address the way my makers are doing their exploration. You are concerned because I have no soul, but I do have a purpose. I am a machine made in the likeness of humans, because only I could stand the pressures of space travel from my own planet. I am programmed in all that I am to do before I am put on board the craft. Only when I have landed safely on your planet, or any other that I have been sent to, do I become conscious and begin my work.

"Because of the way I am made, I have a life expectancy of more than five hundred of your years. I am always the age I look when made. I do not appear to look older over time unless I create that look with makeup, which so far I have not had to do. We maintain privacy as much as is possible. I can be destroyed any time my makers decide my usefulness is over. I cannot reproduce, though I have the workable sex organs of a male human. I do not look for sex, but when it becomes available I use it. Because I can read minds I am aware when a female desires me.

"I can make mistakes. Because I am programmed to use mental telepathy, I sometimes attempt conversations with people in that manner, forgetting they cannot communicate that way. After staring at them for a few minutes I usually get a look that would freeze water. I just smile and walk away. I know quite well what they are thinking. Sometimes people are polite when they talk to me, but what they are saying conflicts with what they are thinking. There are times I wish I had a mother so I could tell them that she was married.

"Violence is something that is foreign to my makeup. I am programmed to be very quiet in violent situations. I can only use force to protect myself from harm. Often, during a disturbance, it only takes a grasp of my hand on an arm or shoulder to quiet the offending person. This is because I have tremendous strength and can use it. My grip is usually enough to get respect. Because I can read minds, I know ahead of time what a violent person proposes to do, and it is a small matter to avoid him or her.

"I was made to listen and observe so I am very quiet and observant when in a group of people. I usually stay in the background away from the people when possible.

This has given me a reputation for being shy and retiring when amongst people whom I have befriended for my own purposes.

"The information that I gather is sent by telepathy to a central bank where the information is analyzed and prepared to send back to the galaxy where I came from. There, it is again analyzed and then filed into another memory bank under past, present, and future. It is used when necessary to give our scientists a completed picture of this galaxy and of its inhabitants.

"My makers are living at a much slower pace than you do here. Time seems to move very slowly there. The days are longer and nights shorter. Everything is precise and methodical. No one hurries to do the simplest task.

"My makers do not have the same appearance that you do. Their bodies are tall and slim with very large heads. There are very few machines in their lives. They have no computers as you have.

"The type of computers they do have are built like me—humanoids with superior knowledge built into them. They are not mobile like me, but are in rows of stationary modules. We have no forests or greenery of any kind. The growth there is more like mushrooms and other spore-like creatures. My makers do not eat as you do, but absorb nourishment through their skin as needed. They do not breathe as you do, but they live in a very humid moist atmosphere made up of chemicals not known here. They would not survive in your world, nor would you in theirs.

"In the long ago past, they did send other forms of creatures to your world as explorers, not knowing the predominant life form in your galaxy. This caused great concern among the inhabitants of your world, and today they still talk about this in books which are considered by you to be fairy tales or myths. Later, when they had found out what the human species of your world looked like, they copied it and then sent ones like me that look like you.

"There are so many mentions, historically, in your Bible, Koran, and other religions about these visits. Even the aboriginals have stories about strange looking visitors amongst them. In every case these visitors gave information and help to make your ancestors more civilized and gave instructions on how to make living conditions better. Usually these were met with success at the beginning, but soon things deteriorated when they began to be worshiped by the humans.

"My makers are very spiritual people and they believe in a Supreme Being. This same belief is common throughout the Universe and the cosmic laws are obeyed without question. The Supreme Being gave the Ten Commandants to everyone in the Universe. To Him we are all one and the same because we are part of Him.

"You have asked me about the Roswell incident that happened a while ago. As I was not there, I only know that which has appeared in the news. I have been told some things by other humanoids and they confirm that something did indeed happen. This is only one crash of space ships. There have been several in different parts of your world. Usually they happen over water and disappear into the sea.

"In this case there were two accidents. First, the craft did crash. Second, the craft did not vaporize as it had been programmed to do. Crucial parts of the power source did explode, but the craft survived and is being secretly examined by your military scientists. The crew of pods stopped working after crashing. One was still working but quit soon after. These humanoids were examined by your scientists. The pods, too, were supposed to vaporize but did not.

"These humanoids have been described many times by people contacted by them in the past, so your scientists knew what they looked like. They examined them but realized they did not have the capability to produce them. They wanted to get the secrets of the spacecraft, but have not yet managed to do so. I know that the propulsion is by magnetic pulsation. It uses the negative and positive of magnetism to create the power. It creates perpetual motion so does not need any further fuel to keep it operating. Simply put, it means that the magnet attracts and repels. So the spacecraft is being pulled and pushed alternately to keep it moving.

"I have told you more than perhaps I should have. I know that in the future there will be contact between humanoids like myself and your government. We have hesitated about this for the past century, realizing the effect it will have on your populace. But because it has been happening over such a long period of time, humans have become used to the concept that other life forms inhabit some of the thousands of galaxies that are in the Universe.

"The political, religious and ethical parts of your lives will be affected. Most people will be able to accommodate the new realizations, but some will not and these will be the problem. There could develop wide-spread panic among these people.

"In any case, for you to survive you must have a new world order. Whether we come or not, this is imperative. You must realize that not only are you one within your world, but you are of the Universe as well. You, Born Many Times, have said this before and explained in the best way you could about the Planes of Consciousness and prophesied the future you all face. But it is still your future to live and accommodate.

"Your scientists have done much in exploring the Universe and outer space. Now it is time for them to explore the inner space. By this I mean micro-space. There are many questions still to be answered in each, but it is more to your advantage to examine micro-space. Already scientists have devised methods of doing this, but there is much more to be done.

"There are many questions waiting to be answered. Do microbes also have microbes? Do germs have germs? Do cells have cells? How small is smallest? How does bacteria become safe from drugs that were successful in eliminating them before? Do they have an intelligence? At the present time in human development, it is much wiser to explore inner space for your benefit. Humans are in a good position balanced between the two spaces, outer and inner, to explore both.

"In the past, humanoids appeared physically among humans, in order to help them. This has been partly successful because your development has increased. Now we are using a different approach. We humanoids, using telepathic means, implant seeds of information, which will be of benefit to humans, into the consciousness of certain people. These seeds of information usually grow into ideas as if they have come from the persons themselves.

"We will continue with this system as long as it proves beneficial to the humans of your world. When we feel that they have progressed as far as we feel they can for their own safety, we will leave them in peace."

Born Many Times was silent a long time and I was sure he had left me. But he began talking again and said:

What this humanoid told me I have repeated to you. You asked me to tell you this, so any problems you have with it are yours. I have no qualms about any information he has given, so I am at peace because I know how well humankind can cope. I have spent all the time that is allowed me to be with you. I will cross your path again in the future, but I will not say where or when. Just remember, the only things cast in stone were the Ten Commandments, and Death is just a word, not a fact.

With that he left me. Suddenly, I felt a loneliness I have never felt before. Something in my life had been taken away. I have spent many hours mulling over our conversations and all that I have learned from them. It is certainly up to the readers to have their own thoughts on all of this. I hope that it will hit a responsive chord and that it will stimulate some serious thinking on their part. Naturally I expect disagreements about this book's contents and even some cries of outrage. I have only repeated what I was told and, like you, I have the right to believe it or not. It was not my intention to offend anyone or to criticize his or her belief systems. Like all things written by man, it is subject to criticism. So be it.

But it is also open for serious discussion. Surely with all our intelligence we can become more aware we are not alone in the Universe. If we are as important as we think we are, is it not time to seriously consider some of the things mentioned in these pages? Serious thought must be given to a world order of some kind and population control.

In conclusion, it is said with some truth that man is the only animal on this Earth that is not useful to the other animals that inhabit it. The only usefulness he can be of now is to try to clean up what he has created, which has been to the detriment of other life forms. This world would be, without a doubt, a better place without the presence of mankind. Ask any animal!

About the Author

George McMullen was born in Woodbridge, Ontario, Canada, on January 14, 1920. Seeking to avoid ridicule, he kept his psychic gifts secret from the public until he was in his forties.

In 1969 he began working with J. Norman Emerson, Ph.D., an anthropologist/archaeologist at the University of Toronto. For more than ten years, from 1969 until Dr. Emerson's death in 1978, the two men did research at various Indian sites in southern Ontario, Ohio, and New York state.

McMullen traveled extensively in Israel, France, England, Mexico, Honduras, and Ecuador. He traveled in Egypt and Iran with Hugh Lynn Cayce of the Edgar Cayce Foundation to research Cayce's statements regarding these areas. His work in Egypt is prominently featured in Stephan Schwarz's books *The Secret Vaults of Time* and *The Alexandria Project*.

Articles about George McMullen have appeared in *Fate*, *Mac Lean Magazine*, and *Canadian Heritage Magazine* to name a few.

He continues to work with archaeologists, criminologists, and psychic explorers. He and his wife Charlotte currently live in British Columbia.

His first book, *Red Snake*, captivated readers with its details of the life of a seventeenth-century Huron. *One White Crow* seeks to shed light on how such a book as *Red Snake* can be authentic. His third book, *Running Bear*, continues the series with the story of the grandson of Red Snake. *Two Faces* completes the chronicle of this Native American family's experience of the White Man's arrival in their land.

Hampton Roads Publishing Company

. . . for the evolving human spirit

Hampton Roads Publishing Company
publishes books on a variety of subjects including
metaphysics, health, complementary medicine,
visionary fiction, and other related topics.

For a copy of our latest catalog,
call toll-free, 800-766-8009,
or send your name and address to

Hampton Roads Publishing Company
134 Burgess Lane
Charlottesville, VA 22902
e-mail: hrpc@hrpub.com
www.hrpub.com